BRIGHTENING THE LONG DAYS

HOSPITAL TILE PICTURES

For my wife Betty
and for children in hospital everywhere

BRIGHTENING THE LONG DAYS
HOSPITAL TILE PICTURES

by
John Greene

Tiles and Architectural Ceramics Society

© John Greene 1987
Published by Tiles and Architectural Ceramics Society 1987

British Library Cataloguing in Publication Data

Greene, John
   Brightening the long days : hospital tile
   pictures.
   1. Tiles—History   2. Hospitals—Design
   and construction
   I. Title   II. Tiles and Architectural
   Ceramics Society
   738.6'09   NK4670

ISBN 0-9512111-0-2

E/115/558–872/W/120387/1030

Produced by Alan Sutton Publishing, Gloucester
Printed in Great Britain

CONTENTS

LOCATIONS

TILE MAKERS MENTIONED IN THE TEXT

BURMANTOFTS, Leeds
BROWN WESTHEAD & MOORE, Hanley, Stoke-on-Trent
CARTER & Co, Poole, Dorset
COPELAND & SONS, Stoke-on-Trent
CORN BROS., Tunstall, Staffordshire
CRAVEN DUNNILL & Co., Jackfield, Shropshire
DE MORGAN, William De Morgan, London and Merton
DOULTON, Lambeth, London
GODWIN, William Godwin & Son, Lugwardine, Hereford
MAW & Co., Broseley and Jackfield, Shropshire
MINTON, and MINTON HOLLINS, Stoke-on-Trent
W.B. SIMPSON & SONS, London
THE MEDMENHAM POTTERY CO.
THYNNE, Hereford

There are also Dutch and English Delft tiles and some tiles by as yet unidentified makers.

Further information on tile manufacturers:

Austwick J. and B.	*The Decorated Tile*, Pitman House 1980
Lockett T.A.	*Collecting Victorian Tiles*, Antique Collectors' Club 1979
Greene Betty,	The Godwins of Hereford, *Journal of the Tiles and Architectural Ceramics Society*, 1982
Van Lemmen Hans,	*Tiles, A Collector's Guide*, Souvenir Press 1979
Atterbury Paul and Irvine,	*The Doulton Story*, Royal Doulton 1979
Catleugh Jon,	*William De Morgan Tiles*, Trefoil Books 1984
Hawkins Jennifer,	*The Poole Potteries*, Barrie and Jenkins 1980
Ray A.	*English Delftware Tiles*, Faber and Faber 1973
Barnard J.	*Victorian Ceramic Tiles*, Studio Vista 1972

ARTISTS AND DESIGNERS NAMED IN THE TEXT

CARTERS
Harold Stabler
Dora M. Batty
Joseph Roelants
James Radley Young
E.E. Stickland
Phyllis Butler

DOULTON
William Rowe
J.H. McLennan
Margaret E. Thompson
Ada Dennis
William J. Neatby
Molly Brett

SIMPSON
Philip H. Newman
Gertrude Bradley
Reginald Watt

MAW
Charles Henry Temple
Walter Crane
Edward Ball

DE MORGAN
William De Morgan

MINTON
J. Moyr Smith
Ann Yeames

Peter O'Brien
Thomas Derrick
Hadyn Jensen
Rosie Smith

ILLUSTRATIONS

COLOUR

BLACK AND WHITE

The author wishes to thank the Publications Panel of the King Edward's Hospital Fund for London for a generous grant towards the cost of producing this book.

Late acknowledgement.
The author would also like to thank the Shaw Hereford Tile Group and W.B. Simpson and Sons Ltd for their contributions towards the cost of publication.

INTRODUCTION

Ceramic tiles have been used for centuries to decorate public buildings and the residences of important people. In this country cathedrals and other religious houses had floors of decorative encaustic tiles, i.e. plain red tiles with an inlay of white clay showing designs of religious scenes, coats of arms, and symbolic pictures of animals, birds and fishes. With the suppression of the monasteries the art of making encaustic tiles was lost until Samuel Wright and Herbert Minton rediscovered it in the 1830s. Tile making became a major industry in the Victorian period as new and advanced techniques were developed for producing other kinds of tiles for floors and walls and for decorating architectural features. The easily cleaned surfaces of glazed tiles were much in demand during the great public health drive to reduce infection in hospitals and public buildings.

Towards the end of the nineteenth century, it became fashionable to brighten the plain tiled walls of children's wards with colourful tile pictures of nursery rhymes, fairy tales and other subjects which would interest and amuse sick children. Well-known tile manufacturers employed famous designers and artists and produced results of high quality until the second world war brought the industry to a halt.

In February 1982 I began a study of ceramic tile pictures in hospitals. I was becoming increasingly concerned about the disappearance of a number of features of architectural and historic interest because of reconstruction of wards, closure of hospitals and demolition of buildings. As a member of the recently formed Tiles and Architectural Ceramics Society I realised that tile pictures could be rescued, conserved and displayed anew as at St Thomas', or resited in a completely new building like Charing Cross Hospital. I wondered to what extent tile pictures had actually been used in hospitals and I decided to seek information about them, and began by reading the tiny amount of literature on the subject. Preliminary letters, telephone calls and visits soon brought the realisation that making a comprehensive record of hospital tile pictures in situ would be a long and expensive task.

A hospital ward, whether occupied by patients and busy staff, altered to serve some other function such as offices or stores, or closed ready for demolition is not the easiest of places in which to measure, describe, photograph and record tiles. I would be glad to hear of any errors or omissions in my results.

In response to two *Blue Peter* programmes on BBC TV I received about 200 letters from both children and adults, some guiding me on to completely new tracks.

Almost all the tiles I am describing in this study are a standard 6 × 6 inch size, making up pictures anything from a two tile (6 inch × 1 foot) rectangle to a massive 10 × 8 foot panel or, in a few cases, complete walls. Nearly all the decoration is under-glaze, i.e. the tile is made, painted, glazed and fired one or more times. This gives a smooth permanent surface.

In some paintings the artists and/or manufacturers have signed their products. Others can be identified because of similarities in style and technique. Only occasionally are pictures duplicated: even in treatments of the same subject there are usually differences in details such as clothes and landscapes.

In this account of my work I have included historical facts about the hospitals because in many cases the details have come from little known sources and by personal communication.

The use of italics in the text represents an actual quotation from the tiles or from literature.

In the space of four years I have collected information from over seventy hospitals and I believe that I have now come to the end of my searches. I would like to thank the King Edward's Hospital Fund for London for a grant which enabled me to meet a lot of the expenses of correspondence, travel and photography. The administrators and nursing staff in the vast majority of hospitals have been generous in assisting me with verbal and written information, and I am grateful for their hospitality and for the time they have given in answering my questions.

The photography of tiles calls for considerable expertise, and I am also grateful to the several hospital photographers and other people who have kindly supplied me with transparencies and colour prints. Hospital and ceramics archivists and historians, members of the Tiles Society and people involved in the BBC *Blue Peter* programmes have all helped me and although I cannot possibly mention everybody by name I would particularly like to say that out of 200 viewers who responded, four children sent letters which led to new discoveries. They are Tamsyn Baxter of Stamford, William Benny of Cromer, Julia Crawley of Hemel Hempstead and Christine Richards of Stockport. Lastly I would like to thank my wife, Betty, (herself engaged in a separate piece of tile research), for her helpful criticism and encouragement.

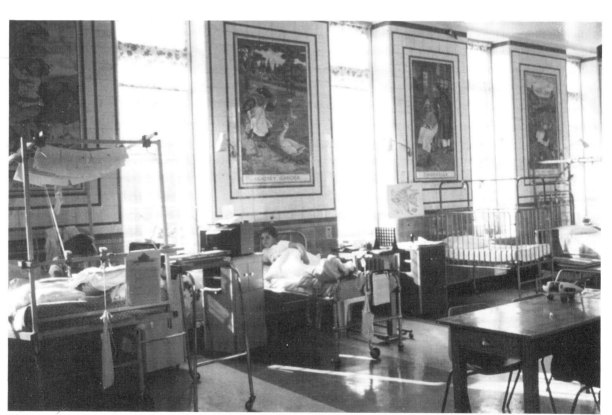

The Louisa Cary Ward, Torbay Hospital

THE CATALOGUE

THE LORD MAYOR TRELOAR HOSPITAL
ALTON, HANTS.

FIREPLACES IN EIGHT WARDS – CARTER.

The hospital is named after its founder, Sir William Purdie Treloar, the son of a Cornishman who became Lord Mayor of London in 1906. He was interested in helping crippled and poor children in the City of London and with the assistance of King Edward VII and Queen Alexandra and many other distinguished persons and influential organisations, he raised the sum of £70,000 to buy the old wooden military hospital at Alton.[1] The Lord Mayor Treloar Hospital grew from this beginning to become one of Britain's best known orthopaedic hospitals.

The decorative tiles occur in the large fireplaces in Wards 1 to 8. Individual picture tiles and groups of four tiles form larger pictures which are set against plain backgrounds. The subjects featured are farmyard animals, farmyard scenes and a Dutch couple engaged in domestic activities. The farmyard pictures are the work of E.E. Stickland and were probably designed around 1925. The Dutch figures are the work of Joseph Roelants, a Belgian artist, who worked for Carters between the wars. The wards date from 1930 when a major new building programme was begun and the Princess Royal Block was opened by His Royal Highness the Duke of Kent.

EIGHT TILED FIREPLACES

WARD 1. Stylised flowers and geometric border (6 × 1 inches).
Centre picture of girl milking a cow and a man with a pail, made up of four 6 × 6 inch tiles by E.E. Stickland.
Four individual tiles showing two people in Dutch costume doing seasonal tasks. Joseph Roelants.

WARD 2. Centre picture of hens in a farmyard. E.E. Stickland.
Individual tiles of people in Dutch costume. Joseph Roelants.

WARD 3. Centre picture of ducks and geese in a farmyard.
Single tiles of ducks, hens, and a turkey. E.E. Stickland.

WARD 4.   Centre picture of cows grazing. Singles of sheep, pigs, rabbits and a horse. E.E. Stickland.

WARD 5.   Twelve tiles geometrically arranged against a plain background with sheep, ducks, farmyard, rabbits, hens, goat, horse, turkey and dove. E.E. Stickland.

WARD 0.   A repeat of Ward 5. E.E. Stickland.

WARD 7.   Centre picture of geese and ducks. Single tiles of ducks, hens, rabbits and a turkey. E.E. Stickland.

WARD 8.   Centre picture of a Dutch girl. Joseph Roelants. Single pictures of pigs, sheep, geese and doves. E.E. Stickland.

BEDFORD GENERAL HOSPITAL
KEMPSTON ROAD, BEDFORD

NURSERY RHYMES AND FAIRY TALES – SIMPSON

Bedford County Hospital was built in 1898 in place of the earlier Bedford General Infirmary. Herbrand, Duke of Bedford, was the Patron and Samuel Whitbread Esq. the President, and their names headed the subscription list with a generous £5000 each. The architect was H. Percy Adams who planned many hospitals. A commemorative booklet[2] gives quite a detailed history of the hospital and contains early photographs of the building and some of the wards. One paragraph describes the tiling in the children's ward:–

> The Children's Ward or Victoria Ward is of the same dimension as the other wards except that it is three feet narrower and is designed for sixteen cots. The upper surfaces of the walls are lined with tiles and are decorated at intervals with artistically painted panels illustrating old Nursery Rhymes and Tales. This work was generously subscribed for by sixteen ladies in commemoration of the Queen's Jubilee. The names of the ladies appear on a Tablet over the entrance door.

The tiles were probably made by Maw's, and the decoration of the panels was by W.B. Simpson and Sons; one of them bears the logo W.B.S. & S. and the date 1898. The artist and designer of the picture panels was Philip H. Newman who is also associated with tile pictures in Cardiff Royal Infirmary. The panels are in good condition in spite of extensive ward alterations, and are some of the best examples of early ceramic art work in children's wards. Inside, over the entrance to the ward, is a tiled dedication panel.

VICTORIA WARD

The tiling of this Ward was undertaken in commemoration of the sixtieth year of Her Majesty's reign by the following ladies:–

Madeline Agnew ALLEN
Geraldine Agnew ALLEN
Amelia Elizabeth BARNARD
Marion BELCHER
Eleanor CARROL
Violet Helen FARRAR
Hester Periam HAWKINS
Agnes Eliza KINSEY
1837

Catherine Mabel MARSH
Beatrice Margaret NUTTER
Agnes ROBINSON
Sybil Alice Mary SKELDING
Katherine TALBOT
Emily THORNTON
Bella Charlotte WHITBREAD

1897

The dedication panel is fifteen 6 × 6 inch tiles wide and eight 6 × 6 inch tiles deep.

THE PICTURES
Eighteen 6 × 3 feet; two 6 × 6 feet.
CINDERELLA AND THE PRINCE – THE GLASS SHOE
WHITTINGTON AND HIS CAT
THE HOUSE THAT JACK BUILT
GOOSEY GOOSEY GANDER
MOTHER HUBBARD
JACK HORNER
DING DONG BELL
WOMAN AND PIG
HUSH A BYE BABY (Colour Plate)
DICKORY DOCK
HUMPTY DUMPTY
RIDE A COCK HORSE
SEE SAW
BO-PEEP
SING O SIXPENCE
MISS MUFFET
JACK AND JILL
SIMPLE SIMON
HEY DIDDLE DIDDLE
MISTRESS MARY

BIRMINGHAM GENERAL HOSPITAL, STEELHOUSE LANE

TILED AREA AND ARCHITECTURAL TERRACOTTA FEATURES BY DOULTON AND CO., LAMBETH, LONDON.

This is a sad example of a hospital having been stripped of most of the decorative features. Three female terracotta figures symbolising Medicine, Surgery, and Philanthropy holding up the Lamp of Life and treading under their feet the Serpent of Death, were originally at the entrance to the Administrative Block, and at the patients' entrance are another three monumental figures representing Air, Purity, and Light.[3] The large Out Patients' Department walls were covered with decorations and moulded tiling – unfortunately all the tiled features have been painted over. A dedication plaque in tiling over a doorway shows that the hospital was opened on 7 July 1897 by Princess Christian representing Queen Victoria.

BIRMINGHAM MATERNITY HOSPITAL

INDIVIDUAL PICTURES OF CHILDREN'S GAMES – DELFT

The Delft type tiles are of uncertain date, probably around the turn of the century, and came from the original c. 1905 Maternity Hospital in Loveday Street, Birmingham. They are now in the Intensive Care Baby Unit of the new Maternity Hospital, framed and hanging on a wall in sets of four, four, and two. The pictures show children's games such as playing leap frog, spinning tops, and sledging in the snow. A dedication plaque shows that the tiles were from Loveday Street and were presented to the Baby Unit by Miss N. McManus, Senior Nursing Officer, on her retirement in December 1981.

COLESHILL HALL HOSPITAL, BIRMINGHAM

LARGE AREAS OF TILED FLOORING – GODWIN

Coleshill Hall is a hospital for the mentally handicapped. It was built in 1873 as a mansion for the Digby family. It is a red brick building in the Gothic style.[4] Birmingham Corporation purchased it in 1925 and converted it for the use of mentally handicapped patients. It is now managed (January 1983) by the North Warwickshire Health Authority who take a pride in the grounds and the mansion which is the centrepiece of the hospital.

In the entrance is an area of 4 inch encaustic floor tiling and in the Main Hall a larger area measuring 30 × 20 feet. The decorated tiles have a red clay body with yellow inlaid designs of lions, fleurs de lys, and flowers. These are set with plain red tiles to form geometric patterns in the style of Victorian cathedral and church floors.

The tiles are in excellent condition in spite of constant heavy use. The administrator was pleased to know the identity of the makers so that he could find replacements for a few broken tiles. The patients took a lively interest when I was recording and drawing a plan of the tiled floors.

BOSCOMBE HOSPITAL, SHELLEY ROAD, BOURNEMOUTH

NURSERY RHYMES, FAIRY TALES AND CHILDREN'S ACTIVITIES – SIMPSON

The Children's Ward was opened by Sylvia, Dowager Countess of Malmesbury on 1 May 1911. The construction was by Messrs. Miller and Sons to plans prepared by the Boscombe Hospital Architect, G.A. Bligh Liversay FRIBA. The ward was the gift of Walter Child Clark who gave many thousands of pounds to charitable institutions and whose name was inscribed on the town's Roll of Honorary Freeman.

In addition to the sixteen beautiful tile pictures there is a dedication panel made by Simpsons.

A.D. 1910
This Ward was given by WALTER CHILD CLARK of
Michelgrove House in this town.
To commemorate a truly noble deed the Committee
of the Hospital have erected this tablet.

The ward is now used as a day hospital ward. The pictures are carefully preserved and highly treasured by an enthusiastic hospital staff. Student Nurse Marian Barnes undertook local historical research for me, Sister Lorna Wellstead photographed the panels, Nurse V. Holme wrote a letter, and a former nurse wrote me a vivid account of her first night duty on the ward full of sick children and how night-time fears were allayed by the pleasant tile pictures on the walls.

The tiles are in excellent condition, and the conservation staff of Ironbridge Gorge Museum have been able to refer to them for details when restoring similar panels for Charing Cross Hospital.

1. Dedication to the benefactor of the ward 4 feet × 3 feet
2. *THE GOLDEN GOOSE* 6 feet × 4 feet (Colour Plate)
3. *SING A SONG O' SIXPENCE* 6 feet × 4 feet
4. *LITTLE BOY BLUE* 6 feet × 2 feet 9 inches
5. *GOOSEY GOOSEY GANDER* 6 × 2 feet 9 inches.
6. *WHERE ARE YOU GOING MY PRETTY MAID* 6 feet × 2 feet 9 inches.
7. *THE BABES IN THE WOOD* 6 feet × 2 feet 9 inches.
8. *APPLE GATHERING* 6 feet × 2 feet 9 inches.
9. *BRINGING HOME THE MILK* 6 feet × 2 feet 9 inches.
10. *CHANGING PASTURE* 6 feet × 2 feet 9 inches.
11. *DAFFODIL GATHERING* 6 feet × 2 feet 9 inches.
12. *GATHERING FUEL* 6 feet × 2 feet 9 inches.
13. *FEEDING THE POULTRY* 6 feet × 2 feet 9 inches.
14. *THE COTTAGE GARDEN* 6 feet × 2 feet 9 inches.
15. *MAYTIME* 6 feet × 2 feet 9 inches.
16. *BUTTERCUPS AND DAISIES* 6 feet × 2 feet 9 inches.
17. *GLEANING* 6 feet × 2 feet 9 inches.

APPLE GATHERING.

BRISTOL ROYAL INFIRMARY

TILED FIREPLACE AND OVERMANTEL – WILLIAM DE MORGAN

This beautiful fireplace is in the entrance hall of the King Edward VII building of Bristol Royal Infirmary. The date of the building is 1912.

A tiled panel on the chimney breast of the fireplace is made up of eighteen 6 × 6 inch tiles with a border of 6 × 3 inches. Besides the actual fire place there are two panels 3 feet × 1 foot 6 inches with a border of 6 × 2 inch tiles.

Each set of tiles makes a panel, Persian in style, mainly in shades of blue and green, with flowers, leaves and swirling stems – all three panels are different but harmonious.

The designs are typical of the work of William De Morgan whose tiles are well known and highly valued. He was associated with William Morris and the Arts and Crafts Movement and in addition to tiles he produced a large amount of pottery which is much sought after by collectors.

THE QUERNS HOSPITAL, CIRENCESTER, GLOUCESTERSHIRE

FRAMED TILE PICTURES – MINTON; B.W. & MOORE; COPELAND (?)

When the Watermoor Hospital, Cirencester's old workhouse closed in the 1970s, six framed picture tiles were found in the Matron's office. They were taken to the new Geriatric Hospital and displayed in a glass case in the entrance area of the hospital. Unfortunately there is no record of how they came to be in Watermoor Hospital but they are most unusual and interesting.

THE PICTURES:–

1. A 16 × 10 inch tile with an underglaze painting in brilliant colours. Six men with shoes discarded, and wearing what appears to be Turkish costumes, are doing a vigorous Dervish dance. Back marks include crude hatching and a tiny impression of the name MINTON.

2. A 6 × 10 inch tile with a picture of two men in Arab dress in conversation by a Mosque type building. The back marking is similar to an illustration of a Copeland tile in J. & B. Austwick's book, *The Decorated Tile*. No. 25 page 132.

3. Three 8 × 8 inch tiles by Minton, Stoke on Trent, showing

Cinderella fitting the missing shoe.
Old King Cole being played to by three fiddlers.
Sing a Song O' Sixpence, the King opening the Pie.
All three show the characters in Elizabethan dress.

4. A 8 × 8 inch tile with a couple kissing by a stile leading to a woodland. Overglaze painting in bright colours. The title printed in French means There is always one who kisses and one who offers the cheek.
Back Mark:– Brown Westhead & Moore & Co. Ravenscroft Patent (2) and initials F C or E K.

CROMER DISTRICT HOSPITAL

ANIMALS – MINTON

The foundation stone of Cromer Hospital was laid by Constance, Lady Battersea, on 16 October 1930. The official opening was performed by Evelyn, Lady Suffield, on 20 July 1932. The architects were Edward Boardman and Son of Norwich, and H. Bullen of Cromer was the builder.

Plesaunce Children's Ward is a memorial to Constance, Lady Battersea, 1843 – 1931. The ward is unusual in that the walls are tiled from floor to ceiling with 8 × 8 inch tiles. The background colour is in subtle shades of pale green and the decorations consist of exotic birds, animals, reptiles, and fish in brilliant colours.

Some of the subjects are within the area of one tile, others span several tiles and the whole scheme is extremely attractive and must give much pleasure and stimulate the interest of sick children.

The variety of subjects include parrots, owls, kookaburras, storks, gulls, flamingos, penguins, herons and other exotic birds; four elephants, two tapirs, three snakes, giraffe, tigers and leopards, seals and brightly coloured fish.

There are no marks to indicate the artist or manufacturer of the tiles but they are in the style of Mintons in both background colour and artistic skill.

DERBYSHIRE CHILDREN'S HOSPITAL

NURSERY RHYME PICTURE TILES – CRAVEN DUNNILL
FRIEZES AND INDIVIDUAL TILES – MAKER UNKNOWN

Until 1877 there were only twelve beds for sick children and these were in the General Infirmary with no provision made for children under the age of 7. The Medical Officer of Health in his Report of 1877 stated that 24 per cent of child deaths occurred in the first year, and children under five accounted for 39 per cent of total deaths. On 9 August that year, leading citizens of Derby gathered to discuss opening an *Institution which shall minister to the sufferings of childhood*.[5] The foundation stone was laid by Mr. M.T. Bass M.P. on 11 July 1882 and the new hospital was opened by Lady Burdett on 2 November 1883. During the 1930s additional wards were built.

During 1980 several picture tiles were removed from one of the original wards when extending the operating theatre. These were restored by Heritage Tile Conservation in 1985 and have now been returned to the hospital to be displayed once again. Five examples are:–

1. *COCK ROBIN IS DEAD AND LAID IN HIS GRAVE. HUM HA LAID IN HIS GRAVE.* 6 × 6 inches
2. *ALL THOSE NICE APPLES ARE LAID ON A SHELF, IF YOU WANT ANY MORE YOU MUST SING IT YOURSELF.* 6 × 6 inches.
3. *THERE CAME AN OLD WOMAN WHO PICKED THEM ALL UP, HUM HA PICKED THEM ALL UP.* 6 × 6 inches.
4. *COCK ROBIN JUMPED UP AND GAVE HER A KNOCK, WHICH MADE THE OLD WOMAN GO HOPPITY HOP.* 6 × 6 inches.
5. *A SET OF SIX CHILDREN'S GAMES.* Each tile 6 × 6 inches.

WARD 2.
Several longitudinal friezes of tube-lined tiling twenty one inches deep made up of three six inch tiles and three inch border tiles against a background of plain tiling. Trees, houses and landscapes in rich colours in Art Nouveau style. (4 feet 6 inches × 1 foot 9 inches)
WARD 4.
32 individual tiles of birds and animals as at Preston. (6 × 6 inches)
WARD 5.
32 individual tiles of birds and animals. (6 × 6 inches)
WARD 6.
34 individual tiles of elephants, tigers, penguins etc. (6 × 6 inches)
WARD 7.
40 individual tiles of similar subjects. (6 × 6 inches)

HERRISON HOSPITAL, DORSET

FIREPLACES – MINTON HOLLINS

The main building of Herrison Hospital for the mentally ill was opened in 1860, as the Dorset County Asylum. Additional wards were added in the period 1870 – 1880. In these later wards, now called the Bourne Unit and made up of Toller, Radipole, Bourne, and Hillfield Wards, there are fifteen fireplaces beautifully decorated with series of Minton Hollins tiles.

All the fireplaces are of similar size and the scheme for each consists of an upper series of five 6 × 6 inch tiles showing for example, Shakespearean scenes, sporting dogs etc., with a motif on each corner, and side panels of four tiles each with different designs. All the main series are of registered designs dated to the 1880s and I have been delighted to find that nearly all of them are listed and numbered in *Minton Hollins Picture Tiles, a Catalogue Raisonné*, by Hans Van Lemmen 1984 – revised 1985.[6] This is probably the best collection of decorated fireplaces of that period by one firm and the hospital authorities are to be congratulated on having preserved these architectural features during various schemes of altering and upgrading the wards. Only one series can be attributed to an artist with certainty – Nursery Rhymes to J. Moyr Smith.

FIREPLACE 1. NURSERY RHYMES. THE QUEEN OF HEARTS, HUMPTY DUMPTY, KING COLE, MISS MUFFET, JACK SPRAT.

FIREPLACE 2. FARMYARD SCENES AND ANIMALS.

FIREPLACE 3. SHAKESPEAREAN SCENES. ROMEO AND JULIET ETC.

FIREPLACE 4. COLOURFUL FLOWERS, ROSE, PANSY, CONVOLVULUS ETC.

FIREPLACE 5. WARBLERS, BUNTING.

FIREPLACE 6. AESOP'S FABLES.

FIREPLACE 7. SPORTING DOGS, SETTER, POINTER ETC.

FIREPLACE 8. THE SIGNS OF THE ZODIAC.

FIREPLACE 9. HUNTING AND RACING SCENES.

FIREPLACE 10. SHAKESPEAREAN SCENES – MERCHANT OF VENICE ETC.

FIREPLACE 11. CLASSICAL WOMEN'S HEADS

FIREPLACE 12. BLUE BIRDS.

FIREPLACE 13. CLASSICAL WOMEN'S HEADS SURROUNDED BY FLOWERS, FRUITS ETC.

FIREPLACE 14. DOMESTIC ANIMALS – HARE, GEESE, TURKEY, COCK AND HEN, DUCK AND DUCKLING.

FIREPLACE 15. MONTAGE OF FIGURES, ANIMALS, BIRDS AND FLOWERS.

EXMINSTER HOSPITAL, EXETER, DEVON

A COLLECTION OF SEVEN INDIVIDUAL PICTURE TILES – COPELAND AND UNKNOWN MAKER.

Exminster Mental Hospital was built in the middle of the nineteenth century and is one of the most architecturally interesting hospitals of that period of mental hospital building.

Ward 12 is in one of the blocks which was added in 1887. When the ward was undergoing upgrading and redecoration in recent years a large number of picture tiles were removed. Many are now in private hands but fortunately seven good examples have been preserved and are in the keeping of the administrator.

The year 1887 marked the Golden Jubilee of Queen Victoria's reign and one of the tiles commemorates the event. Four are from a well known series of Medieval Musicians.

1. Musician playing cymbals with tree on either side. Copeland 6 × 6 inches.
2. Musician playing a violin. Copeland 6 × 6 inches.
3. Musician with a Mandolin type instrument. Copeland 6 × 6 inches.
4. Musician playing a flat Harp type instrument. Copeland 6 × 6 inches.
5. Tile with the Royal Insignia of Queen Victoria, the figures 1887 marking the Queen's Golden Jubilee. Unknown 6 × 4 inches.
6. & 7. Two tiles with floral designs. Unmarked 6 × 3 inches.

GARSTON MANOR MEDICAL REHABILITATION CENTRE, GARSTON, HERTS.

PLAIN AND DECORATIVE TILING – MAKER UNKNOWN

Garston Manor is reputed to have been a hospice attached to St. Albans Abbey which came into the possession of the Crown on the dissolution of the Monasteries.

The present house was built in three stages; the western end in 1812, the middle section between 1842 and 1871, and the large square block at the eastern end rebuilt and added in 1921.

Garston Manor was acquired for the National Health Service in 1950. *In 1968 Garston Manor became the first and only comprehensive medical and industrial rehabilitation centre in Great Britain.[7] In 1974 the DHSS designated Garston Manor in association with the Middlesex Hospital one of a number of Demonstration Centres which are intended to act as a focus of rehabilitation services . . .*

During 1978 an Assessment Unit was built with financial help from the King Edward's Hospital Fund for London . . .

(Extracts from some Historical Notes on Garston Manor.)

1. A tiled entrance hall.
2. Tiled lobby and cloakroom.
3. Persian style tiles in the lounge.

ST HILDA'S HOSPITAL, HARTLEPOOL

NURSERY RHYMES, FAIRY TALES AND A LANDSCAPE – MAW

The tile pictures were in the Children's Ward of the Morison Wing which was opened in 1927 as an extension of the original building of 1865. St Hilda's gained the unpleasant distinction of coming under fire in the First World War in December 1914 when German battleships bombarded a nearby shore battery, causing several casualties.[8] The hospital has now closed but the tile pictures have been rescued and restored by Heritage Tile Conservation before being re-sited in the new District Hospital.

They are signed by Edward W. Ball, thus confirming that the manufacturers were Maw & Co. for whom Ball worked as an artist and designer. They are all 2 feet 3 inches × 2 feet 9 inches.

LITTLE BOY BLUE   EDWARD W. BALL
OLD KING COLE   EDWARD W. BALL
TOM THE PIPER'S SON   EDWARD W. BALL
OLD MOTHER HUBBARD EDWARD W. BALL
JACK AND JILL   EDWARD W. BALL
A MARE AND FOAL   EDWARD W. BALL
DICK WHITTINGTON   EDWARD W. BALL

THE BUCHANAN HOSPITAL, ST. LEONARDS-ON-SEA, HASTINGS

NURSERY RHYMES, VIRGIN AND CHILD, AND LOCAL SCENE – DOULTON
ONE TILED FIREPLACE – MINTON

There are eight framed tile pictures in the Outpatients' Department. They were removed from the Children's Ward in a wing which was the gift of Mrs Thomas Mason. A dedication plaque of eighteen 6 inch tiles shows that the wing was opened on Saturday, 28 November 1908 by Sir George Truscott, Lord Mayor of London. I understand that children from London used to convalesce at the hospital.

   One title panel *Blow Wind Blow* is dedicated to the memory of Annie Cash Ponsford, Matron of the hospital from 1892 – 1906. Another, *Prince Cornwallis*, showing a child astride a large dog on the beach, was given by the dog's owner, Bert Sharpe, Esq. A legend claims that *Prince Cornwallis* saved a child from drowning but it is more likely that the dog carried a collecting tin and raised large sums of money for the Children's Ward. The *Virgin and Child* panel is now in the Chapel and dedicated *to the memory of Dorothy Maude Seaman, 20th July, 1912.*

A further panel *Daffy-down-Dilly* was badly damaged on removal, but it has now been restored at Ironbridge Gorge Museum and returned to the hospital.

The artist was Margaret Thompson of Doultons.

In Louise Ward there is an interesting tiled fireplace with eighteen 6 inch picture tiles representing traditional trades and crafts, designed by J. Moyr Smith for Mintons in the 1870s.

OUTPATIENTS' DEPARTMENT

1. *BLOW WIND BLOW In memory of Annie Cash Ponsford, Matron 1892 – 1902. M.E. Thompson. 4 × 4 feet.*
2. *LITTLE GIRL, LITTLE GIRL, WHERE HAVE YOU BEEN M.E. Thompson. 4 × 4 feet.*
3. *MARY HAD A LITTLE LAMB M.E. Thompson. 4 × 2 feet.*
4. *PRINCE CORNWALLIS THE RESCUER Given by Bert Sharp Esq, owner of Prince Cornwallis. M.E. Thompson. 4 × 2 feet.*
5. *GOOSEY GOOSEY GANDER M.E. Thompson. 4 × 2 feet.*
6. *ORANGES AND LEMONS M.E. Thompson. 4 × 2 feet.*
7. *DAFFY DOWN DILLY M.E. Thompson. 4 × 2 feet.*
8. *LITTLE BOY BLUE M.E. Thompson. 4 × 2 feet.*

IN HOSPITAL CHAPEL

9. A picture of the Virgin and Child. *In memory of Dorothy Maud Seaman 20th July 1912. JESU MEA SPES. 4 × 2 feet.*

LOUISE WARD FIREPLACE

Industrial trades and crafts on 6 × 6 inch tiles.

1. *SMITH, MS*
2. *BARBER, MS*
3. *STONEMASON, MS*
4. *CARPENTER, MS*
5. *TANNER, MS*
6. *POTTER, MS*
7. *TAILOR, MS*
8. *SHOEMAKER, MS*
9. *SAWYER, MS*
10. *WEAVER, MS*
11. *DYER, MS*
12. *PLUMBER, MS*
13. *PAINTER, MS*

(Detail from Daffy Down Dilly)

15

HAVANT WAR MEMORIAL HOSPITAL, HAMPSHIRE

NURSERY RHYMES – DOULTON

A dedication stone on the entrance to the hospital bears the following inscription:–

This stone was laid by Major General The Right Hon. J.E.B. SEELEY C.B., C.M.G., D.S.O., His Majesty's Lieutenant of the County of Southampton, 11th January 1928.

The tile pictures are in Jubilee Ward, formerly built for children and named to commemorate the Jubilee of King George V and Queen Mary in 1935. It is now occupied by geriatric patients who, I was told, appreciate the pictures just as much as the children must have done.

The ten pictures, each 3 × 2 feet, are all familiar nursery rhymes and the name "Doulton" is on the bottom right hand corner of the Little Jack Horner panel. The hospital authorities are interested in their tile pictures, particularly as they have featured in a television programme.

1. *LITTLE MISS MUFFET SAT ON A TUFFET.*
2. *LITTLE BO PEEP HAS LOST HER SHEEP.*
3. *HERE WE GO GATHERING NUTS IN MAY.*
4. *OLD KING COLE WAS A MERRY OLD SOUL.*
5. *LITTLE BOY BLUE COME BLOW UP YOUR HORN.*
6. *OLD MOTHER HUBBARD WENT TO THE CUPBOARD.*
7. *DING DONG BELL PUSSY'S IN THE WELL.*
8. *SEE SAW MARGERY DAW.*
9. *MARY MARY QUITE CONTRARY.*
10. *LITTLE JACK HORNER SAT IN THE CORNER W.R. DOULTON LAMBETH, LONDON.*
    W.R. were the initials of William Rowe who worked at Doultons, 1883 – 1939.

Old Mother Hubbard went to the Cupboard

HEMEL HEMPSTEAD HOSPITAL, WEST HERTS

ANIMAL PICTURES – CARTER

The first hospital in Hemel Hempstead was opened in 1826 under the guidance of Sir Astley Pastor Cooper (Bart). His bust is in the entrance of the present hospital. In 1835 a larger building was needed for which Sir John Sebright (Bart) gave £13,000. By 1877 a new Infirmary for fifty patients was built to meet the needs of an expanding population and this forms the core of the West Herts, Hemel Hempstead Hospital as it is today. Over the years many extensions have been added including the Children's Ward which opened in 1939 just prior to the outbreak of war.[9]

The ward is divided into a number of small units to cater for children suffering from different forms of illness. The lower part of the walls are tiled in an attractive shade of blue and there are ten panels with pictures of animals in human clothing, eight 1 foot 6 inches and two 3 foot 6 inches × 1 foot.

There are proposals for the removal of the tiles to a new site when the hospital closes.

1. FOX
2. PIGLET
3. TORTOISE AND HARE
4. GIRAFFE
5. CAMEL
6. ELEPHANT
7. RHINO
8. OWL
9. DUCK
10. COCK AND HEN

PENKELLY RESIDENTIAL HOME, LUGWARDINE, HEREFORD

DECORATIVE TILES – GODWIN

Penkelly Residential Home for the elderly was at one time the home of William Henry Godwin[10] of the Lugwardine tile-making firm and dates from 1875. There are four large round encaustic tiles on the entrance gateposts, representing the seasons of the year. The exterior of the house is highly decorated with bands of tiling. Godwin tiles were widely used in churches, cathedrals and many public buildings and hospitals.

THE ROUND TILES

1. *SPRING*. White figure of a lady in classical dress holding a spray of flowers against a red background.
2. *SUMMER*. Lady with reaping hook holding a sheaf of corn.
3. *AUTUMN*. Lady plucking grapes from a vine.
4. *WINTER*. Lady warming hands by a fire of sticks.

HESWALL HOSPITAL
A BRANCH OF THE ROYAL LIVERPOOL SICK CHILDREN'S HOSPITAL

ANIMALS AND CHILDREN – CARTER AND MAW
NURSERY RHYMES – UNIDENTIFIED MAKER

When I visited Heswall Hospital in 1984 there was picture tiling in three areas. The building dates from 1907 but the tiling is later. During 1985 the hospital was closed and sold off by the Health Authority. As a result of pressure from me and from Adrian Allen of the Archives Department of Liverpool University it was agreed that the tiling should be rescued and it will hopefully be used again at Alder Hey Hospital for Children in Liverpool.

THE TILING

1. In the Physiotherapy Gymnasium, a former Children's Ward, there was a frieze of two six inch tiles surmounting a tiled dado running round the walls of the room showing children and animals in bright colours. e.g. monkeys at play, animated

18

toys, Dutch children and geese, children by a seashore, a woman and pig, a piper, Punch and Judy show, windmills, etc.
A dedication plaque stated:– *The tiling of this Ward is in memory of Annie Lyall, Highlands, Heswall, 1926.*

2. Ellen Sedgwick Ward had a band of six inch tiles three in depth showing animals in playful mood and Nursery Rhyme characters –

Little Jack Horner
Mary Mary Quite Contrary
There was a Crooked Man
Fiddlers Three
Writing on a tile stated – *given by Roy and Sallie Leach 1934.*

3. Speech Therapy Room. A small frieze of tiling in the style of Carters with domestic animals similar to some in other hospitals.

LEEDS GENERAL INFIRMARY AND OLD MEDICAL SCHOOL

FLOOR AND WALL TILING – MINTON AND BURMANTOFT

The General Infirmary at Leeds was designed by Gilbert Scott and in many ways its Gothic architecture resembles that of St. Pancras Railway Station Hotel. The foundation stone was laid in 1862 and the hospital was opened in 1868, by the Prince of Wales. Florence Nightingale, by then a great authority on hospitals, advised on the design of the wards. An original feature was a large exhibition hall long since demolished, in which the Exhibition of Art was held in 1868, and in which Halle and his Orchestra played.

1. The Long Entrance Corridor.
    This is a large area of encaustic floor tiling, laid in geometric patterns. The borders and backgrounds are of four inch and six inch tiles in plain colours of black, green, red and yellow. In the centre are sets of four six inch tiles forming stylistic patterns of flowers, fleurs de lys, and other designs. This area of floor tiling 60 × 10 feet is attributed to Mintons and is typical of their work in many public buildings.

2. Tiled fireplace in the Board Room.
3. Tiled dado on staircase of the 1927 Nurses' Home.
4. Mosaic tiling in corridor floor of Nurses' Home appears to be made from fragments of encaustic floor tiles probably removed from the Minton entrance corridor.
5. There are small coloured tiles forming geometric patterns on the exterior wall of the main entrance to the Hospital.

THE ADJACENT OLD MEDICAL SCHOOL BUILDING 1894

6. The interior walls of the ornate entrance are elaborately tiled from floor to ceiling with Burmantoft Faience predominantly in shades of green. Over the wide arch of the doorway is the shield of the Yorkshire College adopted by the School of Medicine and the following Latin inscription –

AEGROTOS SANATE LEPROSOS PURGATE.
DONO ACCEPISTIS DONO DATE.
Heal the sick, cleanse the lepers.
Freely you have received, freely give.
(A quotation from Theodore Beza's Latin translation of Matthew 10.8.)

ST. BARTHOLOMEW'S HOSPITAL, LONDON

WALL TILES – MAKER UNKNOWN
DELFT TILES – NOT IN SITU

The plain wall tiles in the Reception and Out Patients area have been painted over but a few decorated tiles have been left exposed and bear the shield of St. Bartholomew's Hospital. Delft tiles which were removed from plunge baths in the South Wing when it was demolished in 1930 are now in the Archivist's store rooms.

According to records held by the Archivist there are 155 single tiles, both Dutch and English, eighteenth century, with a wide variety of designs.[11] Fifteen represent biblical scenes, twenty three are floral, six have Chinese characters, five have animals and twenty four show ships, windmills, buildings and seashore scenes. The remainder are equally interesting.

I was pleased to hear when examining the tiles that there is a possibility of having the Delft tiles restored and resited where they can be seen and admired in a prominent place in the hospital.

BELGRAVE HOSPITAL FOR CHILDREN, LONDON

NURSERY RHYMES – SIMPSON

Belgrave Hospital for Children dates from 1906. The Architects were Adams Holden and Pearson. The three tile panels are in a former Children's Ward which was later used as a rest room for parents visiting children in the hospital. Extensive partitioning to provide cubicles makes it difficult to see the pictures and almost impossible to photograph them. I have not come across the Mulberry Bush panel in any other hospital.

During 1985 the hospital closed but I understand that the tile panels will be rescued and possibly resited in another hospital in the King's College Group of Hospitals.

1. *Goosey Goosey Gander* and full verse (6 × 3 feet) (colour plate)
2. *Little Boy Blue* (6 × 3 feet) (colour plate)
3. *Here we go round the Mulberry Bush* (4 × 3 feet) (cover illustration)

BOLINGBROKE HOSPITAL, WANDSWORTH, LONDON

NURSERY RHYMES – SIMPSON
SMALL TILE PICTURES – CARTER

The tile panels are in the former Children's Ward of the William Shepherd Wing of the hospital. The foundation stone was laid on 9 July 1925 by Princess Mary, Viscountess Lascelles. The wing was opened two years later by Mrs Shepherd and Lady Annie Carmichael.[12] The nursing staff were responsible for raising the money for the thirteen panels of popular nursery rhymes, painted in the style of Mabel Lucy Attwell characters.

In a nearby side ward are a few small tile pictures of animals in human clothing similar to tiling by Carters in a number of other hospitals.

One of the people who helped to make the William Shepherd Wing possible was Sir Bernard Baron, the man after whom the Middlesex Hospital Children's Ward is named.

THE PICTURES

1. *LITTLE BOY BLUE* (4 feet 6 inches × 2 feet 6 inches)
2. *TOM TOM THE PIPER'S SON* (4 feet 6 inches × 3 feet)
3. *SEE SAW MARGERY DAW* (4 feet 6 inches × 3 feet)
4. *MARY HAD A LITTLE LAMB* (4 feet 6 inches × 2 feet 6 inches)
5. *JACK AND JILL* (4 feet 6 inches × 3 feet 6 inches)
6. *HUMPTY DUMPTY* (4 feet 6 inches × 2 feet)
7. *DICKORY DOCK* (5 feet 6 inches × 4 feet 6 inches)
8. *MOTHER HUBBARD* (5 feet 6 inches × 4 feet 6 inches)
9. *LITTLE MISS MUFFET* (4 feet 6 inches × 2 feet)
10. *OLD WOMAN WHO LIVED IN A SHOE* (4 feet 6 inches × 3 feet)
11. *MOTHER GOOSE* (4 feet 6 inches × 3 feet)
12. *SIMPLE SIMON* (4 feet 6 inches × 3 feet)
13. *THE FROG AND THE MOUSE* (4 feet 6 inches × 2 feet 6 inches)
14. TWO BIRDS AND BAMBOO BRANCHES ON A SMALLER PANEL (3 feet 6 inches × 1 foot 6 inches)

IN A SIDE WARD

1. ALLIGATOR IN BLACK TROUSERS AND BLUE COAT (1 foot 6 inches × 1 foot)
2. LION IN BLUE TROUSERS AND GREEN COAT (2 feet 6 inches × 1 foot)
3. MONKEY RIDING AN OSTRICH (1 foot 6 inches × 1 foot)
4. ALLIGATOR IN RED TROUSERS AND GREY JACKET (1 foot 6 inches × 1 foot)

21

CHARING CROSS HOSPITAL

DOMESTIC AND AGRICULTURAL SCENES – SIMPSON

When the old Charing Cross Hospital closed its doors the Hospital Authority called in experts from Ironbridge Gorge Museum to work on the tiles. Six panels were removed in 1978 and 1979 and after restoration were resited in the main entrance area of the new Charing Cross Hospital in Fulham Palace Road. The actual tiles were made by Maws of Jackfield and the decorating, glazing and final firing carried out by Simpsons in their London factory. Simpsons also acted as the London Agents for the firm of Maw.

The tiles are thought to date from the 1890s although some of the same design were installed in Boscombe Hospital in 1912. The Simpson family gave two of the panels. All are 6 feet 6 inches × 3 feet.

1. *THE MILKING LESSON PRESENTED BY F. COLERIDGE SIMPSON*
2. *APPLE GATHERING PRESENTED BY E. GRAHAM SIMPSON*
3. *SOWING PRESENTED BY HENRY HOLLOWAY*
4. *FEEDING THE POULTRY*
5. *PLOUGHING*
6. *HARVESTING*

CHEYNE CENTRE FOR SPASTIC CHILDREN
formerly CHEYNE HOSPITAL FOR SICK AND INCURABLE CHILDREN, LONDON S.W.3

COMMEMORATIVE TILE PLAQUES – MAKER UNKNOWN ? DOULTON

The hospital was founded in 1875 by Mr. and Mrs. Wickham Flower *for the reception of children suffering from chronic and incurable diseases who are on that account excluded or discharged from general hospitals.*[13] An ever increasing demand for admissions led to the opening of the present building on 5 September 1889. In the following June it was visited by the Prince and Princess of Wales after which the Princess became President of the Cheyne Hospital. Children were admitted between the ages of three and ten, and if still in hospital when they reached sixteen they were transferred elsewhere. The majority of children were suffering from diseases of the spine or hip, often accompanied by abscesses, and from diseases of the liver and kidneys. In the first 25 years 480 cases were treated of which 173 died, 142 were cured and 165 were discharged relieved. After the first world war the word 'incurable' was dropped, and general medical and surgical cases were admitted. During the second world war children were evacuated to the country and the hospital became a refugee centre. After the war the idea of a Centre for Spastic Children was projected. The King's Fund, the L.C.C., the S.W. Regional Hospital Board and the Association of Friends co-operated to make it possible to open the Centre in April 1955.

Commemorative tile plaques bear evidence of the generosity of people who endowed cots for children. By subscribing £1000, or £40 a year, a donor was entitled to name a free cot and to nominate an eligible patient for it.

Each plaque is made up of six 6 × 6 inch off-white tiles with a name in good clear lettering surrounded by an oval garland of green oak leaves and acorns, and with a green leaf motif in each corner.

In the ground floor waiting room is an original fireplace with sixteen Dutch polychrome tiles each having a picture of a bird on a green branch, and a lily motif in each corner.

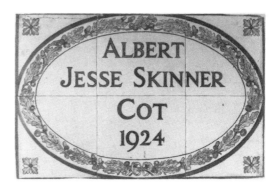

PLAQUES

THE CHARLES KINGSLEY COT 1878
THE WINIFRID COT 1882
THE VIOLET COT 1884
THE DANIEL PIDGEON COT 1901
THE KATIE MACKENZIE FAIRFAX COT 1902
THE ANNIE FAIRFAX COT 1913
VENETIA MEXBOROUGH COT 1917
THE AMY FAIRFAX COT 1920

THE HAZEL ISABEL RAUTHMEN COT 17th April 1923
ALBERT JESSE SKINNER COT 1924
THE HORACE NELSON COT November 1924
THE KATE COURTNEY COT 26th February 1924
ROTARY CLUB OF CHELSEA COT 1931 – 1937

23

CENTRAL MIDDLESEX HOSPITAL, ACTON LANE, LONDON NW 10

NURSERY RHYMES – SIMPSON

The block of Children's Wards of the Central Middlesex Hospital was formally opened on 30 June 1933 by Sir George Newman, Chief Medical Officer of the Ministry of Health. The ward design was described as revolutionary and many visitors came to see it from this country and from overseas. It was three storeys high and in the shape of a ✠ and provided for 104 children's beds and cots. A special feature was the Vita glass windows which could be opened for nearly the whole height, and the flat roof to be used for sun treatment. The walls were said to have picture tiles at eye level and nursery rhyme pictures over the fireplaces.[14]

When I visited in 1982 I was shown five nursery rhyme panels but there was no evidence of the eye level picture tiles.

In March 1985 after an item about Tile Pictures on the *Blue Peter* TV programme I had a letter from a Mr Reginald E. Watt saying that he had painted tile pictures for the Central Middlesex Hospital while working for the firm of W.B. Simpson and Son from 1932 – 1939. When I later called to see him at his home near Portsmouth, he remembered painting pictures of animals and other subjects on individual tiles for the hospital. He was pleased to hear that his Nursery Rhyme pictures were still being admired but sorry to learn that examples of his earliest work could no longer be seen.

THE PICTURES, ALL 4 × 3 feet.

1. RIDE A COCK HORSE
2. THERE WAS AN OLD WOMAN WHO LIVED IN A SHOE
3. SING A SONG OF SIXPENCE
4. LITTLE MISS MUFFET
5. TOM, TOM THE PIPER'S SON

KING EDWARD MEMORIAL HOSPITAL, EALING, LONDON

NURSERY RHYMES, ROYAL PRINCESSES, AND BIBLICAL PICTURE – CARTER

A Cottage Hospital was founded in Ealing in 1871 with the Prince George as its Patron. The present King Edward Memorial Hospital is being replaced by a District General Hospital and it is to the credit of the Health Authority that they called in experts from Ironbridge Gorge Museum to remove a series of tile pictures from the Children's Ward for restoration and re-siting in the new hospital.

In 1934 the Chairman of the Hospital Committee published a booklet at his own expense to commemorate a new Children's Ward. This was presented to child patients *as a souvenir of the Hospital in the hope that you will have good health in the future and will always try to help other children who are ill and may be glad to come into the Hospital.*[15] There followed eighteen pages of pictures of nursery rhymes and verses and a final message *To remember and help the Little Children in the Princess Elizabeth Ward and to ask God each day to make them well.* The booklet also reveals that The Princess Elizabeth Ward *was so named by the generous permission of Their Royal Highnesses The Duke and Duchess of York, who also consented to the erection in the Ward of two Royal pictures in tiles.* One picture shows a thatched cottage with the words *This is the Wonderful Little House which was presented to her Royal Highness The Princess Elizabeth by the Welsh Nation.* The second has the two Princesses standing by a sundial in front of the little house. The Royal pictures were on the entrance wall of the ward and the nursery rhymes were positioned round the ward, above the children's cots. Some of the restored panels have now been re-sited in the new hospital. In May 1985 I visited Miss Phyllis Butler who painted the Royal tile pictures. She was a senior paintress at Carters from 1927 to 1972 and she gave me a detailed account of the painting process and the four firings necessary to provide the finished tile pictures with their fine detail of features, clothes etc.

The pictures were set against a plain background of tiling.

1. *T.R.H. PRINCESS ELIZABETH AND PRINCESS MARGARET ROSE.* 6 feet 6 inches × 5 feet (colour plate)
2. *H.R.H. PRINCESS ELIZABETH'S LITTLE HOUSE.* 6 feet 6 inches × 5 feet
3. *LITTLE MISS MUFFET. THAIN DAVIDSON COT.* 5 × 4 feet
4. *TOM, TOM THE PIPER'S SON. LESLIE MORLEY HORDER COT.* 4 feet 6 inches × 3 feet 6 inches
5. *LITTLE POLLY FLINDERS, QUEEN VICTORIA JUBILEE COT.* 4 feet 6 inches × 4 feet
6. *LITTLE JACK HORNER. ISABEL BEAUMONT SHEPHEARD COT.* 5 × 4 feet
7. *MARY HAD A LITTLE LAMB. THE DANCERS COT.*
8. *JACK AND JILL. LADIES LINEN LEAGUE COT, AND JAMES HENRY WHITTLE.* 8 × 5 feet

9. RIDE A COCK HORSE. MAYOR OF EALING 1914–1915 COT AND W.A. SATCHELL. 8 × 5 feet
10. THE QUEEN OF HEARTS. EALING SPECIAL CONSTABULARY COT. 5 × 4 feet
11. LITTLE BO PEEP. THE HARRINGTON COLLEGE COT. 5 × 4 feet
12. HUMPTY DUMPTY. ST MATTHEW'S CHILDREN'S LEAGUE COT. 5 × 3 feet
13. MISTRESS MARY QUITE CONTRARY. CHARLES SHEPHEARD COT. 5 × 3 feet
14. LITTLE BOY BLUE. ST STEPHEN'S LITTLE FELLOWSHIP COT. 4 feet 6 inches × 4 feet
15. A picture of Christ suffering little children to come to Him. 5 × 4 feet

GUYS HOSPITAL, LONDON

NURSERY RHYMES ETC. – CARTER

When Caleb Diplock Wards on the third floor of Hunt's House in Guys Hospital were no longer used for children the tile pictures were left in situ. On the advice of the expert staff of Ironbridge Gorge Museum the pictures were covered with a coat of paint to preserve them until enough money was available to have them removed, restored and displayed in another site some time in the future.

The pictures are similar to a popular series produced by Carters for hospitals in the 1930s and some are illustrated in a catalogue of their tile pictures.

1.   LITTLE MISS MUFFET
2.   LITTLE JACK HORNER
3.   POLLY FLINDERS
4.   MARY HAD A LITTLE LAMB
5.   LITTLE BO PEEP
6.   THE KNAVE OF HEARTS
7.   TOM TOM THE PIPER'S SON
      (colour plate)
8.   HUMPTY DUMPTY
9.   LITTLE BOY BLUE
10. MARY MARY QUITE CONTRARY
11. ORANGES AND LEMONS
12. JACK AND JILL
13. RIDE A COCK HORSE
14. A CALF
15. TWO CAMELS
16. GOOSE GIRL
17. TWO DEER
18. *TOM, HE WAS A PIPER'S SON*
      and eight others

KING'S COLLEGE HOSPITAL, DENMARK HILL, LONDON

FIREPLACE – DOULTON

The foundation stone of King's College Hospital was laid by His Majesty King Edward the Seventh on 20 July 1909 and the completed hospital was opened by King George the Fifth on 20 July 1913. The architect was W.A. Pite. For a London hospital of that period it is surprisingly devoid of large tile pictures.

However, one fireplace and overmantel in the Out Patients' Department has some small hand-painted tile pictures in the colours, subject and style of the Doulton Nursery Rhyme artist Margaret E. Thompson. Each tile picture consists of two 6 × 6 inch tiles placed one

above the other, bordered by 6 × 2 inch tiles and separated from the next picture by 6 × 4 inch pale green tiles. The pictures on the overmantel are:–

JACK AND JILL WENT UP THE HILL
JACK AND JILL FELL DOWN THE HILL
CINDERELLA ALL ALONE
CINDERELLA AND THE FAIRY
SEE SAW
HIGGELTY PIGGELTY

The tile pictures seem to be totally unknown to most of the hospital staff, except those who work in the Out Patients' Department.

THE KING'S FUND MINIATURE HOSPITAL
NOW IN THE LONDON SCIENCE MUSEUM

NURSERY RHYME TILE PICTURES – SIMPSON

The King's Fund Miniature Hospital Exhibition at the Building Centre, 158 New Bond Street, London, was opened by H.R.H. The Prince of Wales K.G. on Friday 6 January 1933.

In 1929 the Propaganda Committee of the Fund suggested the idea of a scale model, *complete in its smallest details to arouse the interest of the public*. The Royal Institute of British Architects nominated Mr Percy Adams of Adams Holden and Pearson to produce the design and plans. As Mr Percy Adams was associated with many hospitals containing tile pictures by W.B. Simpson and Sons it came as no surprise to read in the Exhibition Souvenir Booklet that:–

> *The top floor shows the Children's Ward and the Kitchen. This Ward, though the same size as the Ward below, is rather differently arranged to suit the needs of childhood. The walls are tiled by W.B. Simpson and Sons and are decorated with Nursery Rhymes adapted from the original cartoons by Thomas Derrick: "Dick Whittington", "Ride a Cock Horse", "Tom, Tom the Piper's Son", "Little Miss Muffet", "Jack and Jill", are among the subjects. The tiles are actual miniature tiles, and in all, including Kitchen etc., 13,000 have been specially made for the Model, and have been through the same process of manufacture as a full-glazed tile.[16]*

The miniature hospital was first mentioned to me by Mr. Lionel Simpson, long since retired from the family tile firm. In May 1985 I visited Mr. Reginald Watt to hear about his time as an artist at Simpsons. He showed me the Miniature Hospital Souvenir Booklet and some of the miniature tiles and confirmed that he had actually designed and painted the Nursery Rhyme tile pictures for the hospital. Mr Watt was an architect by profession and took up work as a ceramic artist during the lean years of the thirties but returned to his original architectural work at the outbreak of the war in 1939.

The King's Fund Miniature Hospital can now be seen in the Wellcome History of Medicine Exhibition on the 4th/5th floors of the Science Museum, in South Kensington.

MINIATURE PICTURES

1. DICK WHITTINGTON
2. RIDE A COCK HORSE
3. TOM, TOM THE PIPER'S SON
4. JACK AND JILL
5. LITTLE MISS MUFFET

THE MIDDLESEX HOSPITAL, LONDON

NURSERY RHYMES, VILLAGE SCENES, AND PET ANIMALS – CARTER

When the West Wing of the Middlesex Hospital was rebuilt in 1930, thousands of yards of tiling were used to line the walls and corridors. Carters of Poole, Dorset, described it at the time as probably their single biggest contract. The principal colour for the corridor tiling was off-white relieved by bands of green with the numbers and names of the wards picked out in good clear lettering. The highlight of the whole scheme was the magnificent and colourful Babies' Ward, later to be named The Bernard Baron Ward. Carters' 1935 Catalogue gives the following useful information:–

> the generous benefactor, Sir Louis Baron, made himself responsible for the decoration of the Ward. He instituted a national competition for a design for its decoration. The fine broad treatment of the adopted design, the work of Mr Hadyn Jensen, called for a technique hitherto unused in tile decoration. Flat masses of bright colours were desired, masses applied in what we think of as the poster manner, so different from the oil or water-colour technique to which we had become accustomed. The result was an outstanding success which led to a series of further experiments on similar lines elsewhere. A technique had been found and it was proved to be the right technique.

The left hand wall has a large nursery rhyme picture mostly obscured by a large cupboard, in the spaces between the windows are brightly coloured pictures of trees, birds, animals and another nursery rhyme. The end wall is spectacular, with a huge picture twenty six feet long and seven and a half feet high. The centre piece is a fairground roundabout entitled *ALL THE FUN OF THE FAIR*.

Beside it is a colourful lady selling balloons, and familiar sideshows like Punch and Judy. The decoration on the right hand wall begins with a windmill and a landscape followed by four nursery rhyme characters filling the spaces between the windows. The whole scene leads to the remaining wall which is filled with swirling Maypole dancers on a village green.

This rare and fine example of tile decoration gave life to the Children's Ward as I saw it in 1982, but I got a very different impression on seeing it again in December 1985. The Ward was closed to make way for an extension to the Operating Theatre, and Hadyn Jensen's imaginative design for the amusement of sick children seems abandoned in the midst of empty beds and ward furniture. However, I found enthusiastic members of the nursing staff planning a campaign to have the pictures rescued before the builders moved in, and I hope they will succeed in their efforts.

THE WARD TILING

1. A PARTLY OBSCURED PICTURE.
2. A COCKEREL. 2 feet × 2 feet 6 inches
3. GOOSE. 2 × 2 feet
4. CAT. 2 feet 6 inches × 2 feet
5. TREE. 3 feet 6 inches × 1 foot 6 inches
6. MONKEY. 2 feet 6 inches × 2 feet
7. SQUIRREL. 2 × 2 feet
8. TREE. 3 feet 6 inches × 1 foot 6 inches
9. HARE. 2 feet 6 inches × 2 feet
10. PARROT. 9 feet 6 inches × 7 feet 6 inches
11. SIMPLE SIMON. 9 feet 6 inches × 7 feet 6 inches
12. *ALL THE FUN OF THE FAIR. HADYN JENSEN DESIGNER 1929.* 26 feet × 7 feet 6 inches (detail colour plate)
13. WINDMILL AND LANDSCAPE. 9 feet 6 inches × 4 feet 6 inches
14. MARY MARY QUITE CONTRARY. 6 × 5 feet
15. LITTLE MISS MUFFET. 6 feet 6 inches × 4 feet 6 inches
16. MARY HAD A LITTLE LAMB. 6 feet 6 inches × 7 feet
17. TOM, TOM THE PIPER'S SON. 5 × 4 feet
18. THE MAYPOLE. 16 feet × 7 feet 6 inches
19. IN LETTERING: – *THE BERNARD BARON CHILDREN'S WARD*

MOORFIELDS EYE HOSPITAL, HIGH HOLBORN, LONDON

NURSERY RHYMES – SIMPSON

Moorfields Eye Hospital was formerly known as the Westminster Ophthalmic Hospital. A sales pamphlet by W.B. Simpson & Sons mentions the supply of tile pictures to the hospital.[17] The hospital was built in the 1930s to the design of the architects Adams Holden and Pearson. The existence of the pictures came to light following a news item in the *Sunday Times* in February 1985. Mr Patrick Trevor Roper, Consultant Ophthalmologist at the hospital, wrote to tell me that some tile pictures were boarded over when the Maud Arran Children's Ward was being divided up about fifteen years ago, but fortunately they had been photographed. He said that the hospital was due for closure and hoped that the pictures could be rescued and given a place in the City Road branch.

Maud, Countess of Arran, was Chairman of the Governors 1910 – 1926.

All the pictures are 5 × 3 feet.

HICKORY DICKORY DOCK
DICK WHITTINGTON
JACK AND JILL WENT UP THE HILL TO FETCH A PAIL OF WATER
LITTLE MISS MUFFET SAT ON A TUFFET, EATING HER CURDS AND WHEY
RIDE-A-COCK HORSE TO BANBURY CROSS – TO SEE A FINE LADY RIDE ON A WHITE HORSE
OLD MOTHER HUBBARD WENT TO THE CUPBOARD, TO GET HER POOR DOG A BONE
TOM, TOM THE PIPER'S SON STOLE A PIG AND AWAY HE RUN
LITTLE JACK HORNER SAT IN A CORNER EATING A CHRISTMAS PIE
THE QUEEN OF HEARTS SHE MADE SOME TARTS, UPON A SUMMER'S DAY
OLD KING COLE WAS A MERRY OLD SOUL
(colour plate)

The Queen of Hearts she made some tarts, Upon a Summers Day.

THE NORTH MIDDLESEX HOSPITAL, SILVER STREET, LONDON N 17

DECORATED TILES – MINTON HOLLINS

The Hospital dates from 1909. The administration office buildings were originally the houses of the Medical Superintendent and the Matron. Both were extensively tiled in Minton Hollins tiling in Art Nouveau style. Some of the tiling was removed during alterations and the administrator kindly gave me six tiles to study. The major part of the tiling is still in situ.

TILES 1 and 2. White bodied tiles curved to provide a smooth corner for walls, and decorated with a tube-lined green leafed climbing plant and yellow flower.
TILES 3 and 4. Two tiles when joined together form a branching plant design.
TILE 5. A stylised yellow flower on the tiled plant 3 and 4.
TILE 6. Similar to Tile 5.

PADDINGTON GREEN CHILDREN'S HOSPITAL, PADDINGTON GREEN, LONDON

TILE PICTURES IN THREE AREAS OF THE HOSPITAL – SIMPSON, DOULTON AND AN UNKNOWN MAKER.

Paddington Green Children's Hospital dates from 1883. The present building has a plaque in the Reception Area which records:–

> THIS HOSPITAL AFTER BEING REBUILT WAS
> FORMALLY OPENED BY HER ROYAL HIGHNESS
> PRINCESS MARY ADELAIDE DUCHESS OF TECK
> ON MONDAY 1st JULY, 1895.

1.   An extract from the Annual Report of that year reads:–

The large Top Ward is beautifully decorated with panels of glazed tiles representing well known Nursery Rhymes. The cost defrayed from a legacy left for the purpose by Miss Charlotte Jones, a valued servant for more than forty years.[18]

Only two of the pictures can now be seen. Top Ward was later named the Princess Louise Ward. It is no longer used for patients and was converted to offices in recent years. One of the pictures is easily identifiable as the work of W.B. Simpson and Sons by the firm's name on the tiles, and the title *This is the House that Jack Built*. The style is similar to the Simpson tile pictures in Bedford General Hospital commemorating Queen Victoria's Diamond Jubilee in 1897. There were probably twenty pictures in all, but I was unable to get in to the false ceiling space to see if the upper portions were visible. A 1901 photograph of the ward confirms that the pictures are identical to those in Bedford.

2.   Reading on from the 1895 Report:–

It is proposed to carry out the same idea in the Lower Ward with subjects selected from the scriptures. Designs have been submitted to the Committee for approval and are on view in the entrance. Eight panels have been already subscribed for at £20 each.

Lower Ward is still in use and named The Mary Adelaide Ward. The ceiling has been lowered and cubicles built to create privacy, and nothing is visible of the pictures. Some older members of the staff remembered the pictures and I was invited to climb into the space above this false ceiling armed with a torch. To my delight I was able to see the upper portion of the tile pictures and identify the following from the printed titles:–

JACOB'S DREAM	*ST JOHN PREACHING*
THE GOOD SHEPHERD	*JOSEPH MEETING HIS BRETHREN*
DAVID AND GOLIATH	*THE FLIGHT INTO EGYPT*
THE BOY SAMUEL	*THE EPIPHANY*
CHRIST BLESSING CHILDREN	*ELIJAH AND THE RAVEN*
THE BABE JESUS	*JOSEPH SOLD BY HIS BRETHREN*
JESUS IN THE TEMPLE	

It is difficult to tell whether the panels were fixed at the time of building or gradually added as donors provided the money. For example, the Report in 1895 said eight panels had already been subscribed for at £20 each. Later Reports mentioned that in 1903 Mr. C.F. Greenhill presented a tile picture leaving only five vacant places. In 1907 Mr and Mrs Pollock gave £25 for *The Epiphany* and in 1910 a further £25 for *The Flight into Egypt*. A Mr George Hanbury gave £30 in 1909 for *Joseph sold by his Brethren* and in 1910 a further £30 for *Joseph meeting his Brethren*.

   The pictures are attributed to Doultons of Lambeth, London, and the firm's little book *Pictures in Pottery* published in 1904 has an illustration of *The Good Shepherd*.[19]

3.   The Small Ward. An 1896 Hospital Report refers to the decoration of the Small Ward with tile pictures the subjects being selected from Aesop's Fables. The cost was defrayed by Mr S.G. Holland who contributed £500 in memory of his daughter.

   I could find no evidence of these pictures nor anybody who could tell me anything about them. The name Stephen Holland occurs in St. Thomas' Hospital where he defrayed the cost of the decorative tiling in memory of his daughter Lilian after whom Lilian Ward was named.

4.   The Out Patients' Department. The Out Patients' Department of Paddington Green Children's Hospital was rebuilt and enlarged and formally opened by Her Royal Highness Princess Louise, Duchess of Argyle on 16 November 1911. The architect was Allen E. Munby. The Hospital Committee Report for 1912 drew attention to the

following matter of urgency the need of further gifts of Tile Picture Panels for the new Out Patients' Department. These pictures represented children's games, nursery stories, country scenes etc., and will serve three useful purposes, viz; to brighten and decorate the walls of the waiting room, to interest and distract the children from their sufferings: and also (the panels being washable) to reduce the cost of the annual cleaning. Particulars of the cost of the panels can be obtained of the Secretary. A sketch plan of the complete scheme can be seen in his office.

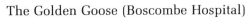
The Golden Goose (Boscombe Hospital)

Hush A'Bye Baby (Bedford General Hospital)

Goosey Gander and Little
Boy Blue (Belgrave
Children's Hospital)

The Princesses (Ealing
Hospital)

Tom, Tom, the Pipers Son (Guys Hospital)

Buy My Balloons. Detail from 'All the Fun of
the Fair' (The Middlesex Hospital)

Old King Cole (Moorfields Eye Hospital)

Snowballing (Paddington Green Children's Hospital)

Dick Whittington (St. Thomas' Hospital)

St. Swithin's Day (Royal Victoria Infirmary,
Newcastle-upon-Tyne)

Proscenium Arch (Detail) (St. Nicholas Hospital, Gosforth, Newcastle-upon-Tyne)

Little Boy Blue (Preston Royal Infirmary)

Royal Coat of Arms (Royal Berkshire Hospital, Reading)

Mary, Mary (West Kirby Residential School)

The Ark (Kent and Sussex Hospital, Tunbridge Wells)

St. David (Cardiff Royal
Infirmary)

Miss Muffet (Southlands
Hospital, Invercargill N.Z.)

Unfortunately I have not been able to find the sketch plan or the details of the cost of the panels. However, fifteen panels show that the appeal was successful as the names of the people who gave them are on the tiles.

1. *THE WHITE STONE POND HAMPSTEAD, MR & MRS ALUN MUMBY*. 5 feet 6 inches × 3 feet 6 inches
2. *PADDINGTON GREEN, F. ANSTEY, ESQ.* 5 feet 6 inches × 3 feet 6 inches
3. *THE PICNIC, THE HON. MRS BOUVERIE.* 4 feet 6 inches × 4 feet
4. *CHILDREN SNOWBALLING, J. BALFOUR ALLAN ESQ.* 5 feet 6 inches × 3 feet 6 inches (colour plate)
5. *DIGGING IN THE SANDS, MRS RAGLEY OWEN AND MISS PUGH.* 3 feet 6 inches × 2 feet 6 inches
6. *AS HAPPY AS A KING, MRS C.A. JAMES.* 4 feet 6 inches × 5 feet 6 inches
7. *PETER PAN, MRS. NOBLE OF PARK PLACE AFTER ARTHUR RACKHAM*
8. *BUILDING, THE SONS AND DAUGHTERS OF THE LATE THOMAS HENWOOD.* 3 feet 6 inches × 1 foot
9. *BABES IN THE WOOD, GEORGE HANBURY ESQ., TREASURER* 5 feet 6 inches × 3 feet 6 inches
10. *SCOUTING, THE PUPILS OF LEINSTER HOUSE SCHOOL PER THE MISSES MANVILLE* 5 feet 6 inches × 3 feet 6 inches
11. *OBSCURED FROM VIEW BY FURNITURE.*
12. *SOWING, FROM THE LITTLE FRIENDS CLUB* 4 feet × 3 feet 6 inches
13. *A MAD TEA PARTY – ALICE'S ADVENTURES IN WONDERLAND* 7 feet × 3 feet 6 inches
14. *FRENCHAY* { *GIVEN BY MR. DOUGLAS OWEN*
15. *FINCHINGFIELD,* { *CHAIRMAN AND MRS OWEN*

Paddington Green Children's Hospital is due for closure in a few years' time. It is hoped that the tile pictures from the Out Patients' Department will be rescued and moved to the new District Hospital.

It is unlikely that the pictures from The Princess Louise and The Mary Adelaide Wards will be saved. Neither of them match those in the Out Patients' Department for attractiveness of colour and subject. However, it would be good to uncover them if the building should continue to be used for some other purpose. Paddington Green has proved to be a fruitful hunting ground for hospital tile pictures.

HEADQUARTERS AND COLLEGE OF THE RICHMOND FELLOWSHIP
8, ADDISON ROAD, LONDON W14 8DL

DECORATIVE TILING – WILLIAM DE MORGAN

The Richmond Fellowship, which occupies 8 Addison Road, is a registered Charity for the Welfare and Rehabilitation of the Mentally Ill. The house was designed for Sir Ernest Debenham around 1904 by the architect Halsey Ricardo. He used beautiful tiles by William De Morgan in both the interior and exterior of the building, most of which is preserved in its original state. The tiling scheme is a well known example of De Morgan's work and is fully documented elsewhere.[20]

ST MARY'S HOSPITAL, PRAED STREET, LONDON

ALICE IN WONDERLAND IN LEWIS CARROLL WARD – MAKER UNKNOWN

The tile picture scenes are from *Alice in Wonderland*, and the ward is a memorial to Lewis Carroll. It was opened in 1937 by Her Majesty the Queen (Queen Elizabeth the Queen Mother) and *Alice*, Alice Meynell, by then a white haired old lady, was there to see it.[21]

The tiles are shaped like pieces of a jigsaw, unlike the usual square ones, and the surface does not have the normal ceramic finish. The pictures are large, with some measuring as much as twelve feet by three feet. One bears the signed initials E.V.B. but I have been unable to trace the artist, and the short history of St. Mary's makes only a brief mention of the pictures.

Curtain rails and cubicles to provide isolation and privacy have obscured some of the text but I have managed to copy parts of the quotations which go with the pictures.

You are old said the youth, one would hardly suppose that your eye was as steady as ever. Yet you balance an Eel on the end of your nose, what made you so awfully clever.

Pepper and vinegar besides are very good indeed. Now if you are ready Oyster, we can begin to feed.

Poor little Lizard Bill was in the middle being held up by two guinea pigs who . . .

An Invitation for the Duchess.

Alice and the White Knight.

The Mad Hatter's tea party.

ST MARY'S HOSPITAL, PLAISTOW, LONDON

NURSERY RHYMES, LANDSCAPES AND SHIPS – MAKER UNKNOWN

The foundation stone was laid by Sir George Truscott, Lord Mayor of London, 1909, the architect being Saxon Snell, and the builder, F. & E. Davey Limited.

St Mary's Hospital is now closed but happily the interesting tile panels which were given by or to commemorate private individuals, local organisations, and people who gave long services to the hospital have been rescued. Unfortunately, a number of the panels were damaged when over-bed lighting was installed in one ward.

Two photographs of the wards in the Annual Reports of the hospital have the following captions:–

THE QUEEN ALEXANDRA WARD.
Named by the kind permission of Her Most Gracious Majesty Queen Alexandra, Patroness.
The walls were decorated with tile pictures, and the tile floor laid, by funds given in response to the Matron's Appeal, 1921.[22]

THE VISCOUNTESS PARKER WARD.
Named in recognition of the generous support and active services of the late Viscountess Parker.
The walls were decorated with tile pictures, and the floor laid, by funds given in response to the Matron's Appeal, 1922.

Miss Ray, the Matron, also raised £12,000 to build and furnish a Nurses' Home and one of the Annual Reports refers to her appeal for a million pennies. It seems strange that the walls were tiled several years after the hospital had been built.

The Alexandra Ward pictures consist of two large panels each made up of seventy-two 6 inch tiles depicting *Jack and Jill* and *Little Boy Blue* and twelve panels of twenty-eight 6

inch tiles which include two Nursery Rhymes, *Good King Arthur*, and *Pat-a-Cake*, which do not occur elsewhere in my study. The pictures in Viscountess Parker Ward almost wholly consist of colourful land-and seascapes. Two Galleon pictures in a side ward are in the style of work by Carters of Poole.

The King Edward's Hospital Fund is recorded as a regular contributor to the funds of St. Mary's Hospital, which appears to have relied heavily upon voluntary support.

The tile pictures were removed from the walls by the experts from Ironbridge Gorge Museum in 1984. After restoration some will be re-sited in the new District Hospital and some will go to Museums.

QUEEN ALEXANDRA WARD. 16 Tiled Panels.

1. *JACK AND JILL* Dedicated to HOLFORD 5 feet 6 inches × 3 feet 6 inches
2. *HUMPTY DUMPTY* Dedicated to ANDREW, PAUL AND RUTH ETC. 2 feet × 3 feet 6 inches
3. *LITTLE MISS MUFFET* Dedicated to C M McKEYTE, J H PINHEY 2 feet × 3 feet 6 inches
4. *PAT-A-CAKE, PAT-A-CAKE, BAKER'S MAN* Dedicated to Mrs ELLA B. STEELE 2 feet × 3 feet 6 inches
5. *LITTLE BO-PEEP* Dedicated to H D HALE and FRIENDS 2 feet × 3 feet 6 inches
6. *OLD MOTHER HUBBARD* Dedicated to MRS E BAKER 2 feet × 3 feet 6 inches
7. *GOOD KING ARTHUR* Dedicated to MR TOM BARNETT 2 feet × 3 feet 6 inches
8. *MARY HAD A LITTLE LAMB* Dedicated to M. K. SEYMOUR 2 feet × 3 feet 6 inches
9. *HICKORY DICKORY DOCK* Dedicated to EAST HAM TELEPHONE EXCHANGE STAFF 2 feet × 3 feet 6 inches
10. *LITTLE JACK HORNER* Dedicated to MR S WAREHAM 2 feet × 3 feet 6 inches
11. *BAA BAA BLACK SHEEP* Dedicated to MRS A L SHEPPARD 2 feet × 3 feet 6 inches
12. *TOM TOM THE PIPER'S SON* Dedicated to ST MARY'S HOSPITAL BRANCH OF CANNING TOWN & POPLAR ETC. 2 feet × 3 feet 6 inches
13. *GOOSEY GOOSEY GANDER* Dedicated to C & K SILLEY 2 feet × 3 feet 6 inches
14. *LITTLE BOY BLUE* Dedicated to CHAIRMAN AND WIFE 5 feet 6 inches × 3 feet 6 inches

DEDICATED
TO THE MEMORY OF
MR. JAMES W.Y. CEARNS.
A RESPECTED MEMBER OF THE COMMITTEE OF
MANAGEMENT OF THIS HOSPITAL.
1919 — 1934

SIDE WARD.

15. SAILING SHIP BEARING ST. GEORGE'S CROSS ON SAIL 5 Tile Dedication to Memory of MR J W Y CEARNS 2 × 3 feet
16. SAILING SHIP BEARING THREE ROYAL LIONS ON SAIL 5 Tile Dedication to Memory of MR W F WHITE 2 × 3 feet

VISCOUNTESS PARKER WARD. 20 Tiled Panels.

17. CASTLE OVER ESTUARY Dedicated to DAVIS 6 feet × 2 feet 6 inches
18. FISHING PORT Dedicated to S.W. HAM MASONIC CLUB 3 feet × 2 feet 6 inches
19. CHURCH OVER FIELD Dedicated to MARTIN 3 feet × 2 feet 6 inches
20. YACHT ON SEASHORE Dedicated to MAIR 3 feet × 2 feet 6 inches
21. BRIDGE OVER RIVER Dedicated to ADAMSON 3 feet × 2 feet 6 inches
22. SEASHORE WITH BATHING MACHINES Dedicated to BIGG 3 feet × 2 feet 6 inches
23. CASTLE OVERLOOKING LAKE AND MOUNTAINS Dedicated to HOGGER 3 feet × 2 feet 6 inches
24. SAILING BOAT BY SEASHORE Dedicated to BIGG 3 feet × 2 feet 6 inches
25. LAKESIDE SCENE WITH CHURCH SPIRE Dedicated to S.W. HAM HORTICUL-TURAL SOCIETY 4 feet × 2 feet 6 inches
26. BOY ON SEASHORE WITH SAILING BOAT Dedicated to S.W. HAM CONSTIT-UTIONAL CLUB 4 feet × 2 feet 6 inches
27. PUNTING ON THE RIVER BY COUNTRY HOUSE Dedicated to PAPILLON 4 feet × 2 feet 6 inches
28. YACHT BY THE SEASHORE Dedicated to the PLAISTOW AND CANNING TOWN DEMONSTRATION COMMITTEE 4 feet × 2 feet 6 inches
29. COUNTRYSIDE SCENE WITH COTTAGE AND CORNFIELDS Dedicated to GOR-BELL 3 feet × 2 feet 6 inches
30. JETTY ON THE LAKESIDE Dedicated to STURTON 3 feet × 2 feet 6 inches
31. LAKESIDE AND MOUNTAIN SCENE Dedicated to RANDALL 3 feet × 2 feet 6 inches
32. YACHT IN CHOPPY SEAS Dedicated to COMMITTEE OF LONDON CALEDONIAN FRIENDLY SOCIETY 3 feet × 2 feet 6 inches

33. FARMHOUSE AND THATCHED BARN Dedicated to SEYMOUR 3 feet × 2 feet 6 inches
34. SHORELINE WITH CLIFFS AND BOAT Dedicated to MACMILLAN 3 feet × 2 feet 6 inches
35. VILLAGE STREET Dedicated to BROOKS 3 feet × 2 feet 6 inches
36. SHORELINE Dedicated to ARCHIE WHITE 6 feet × 2 feet 6 inches

ST THOMAS' HOSPITAL, LONDON

NURSERY RHYMES, FAIRY TALES AND TREES – DOULTON

The panels were in the former Children's Wards, Lilian and Seymour, which were opened for use in 1901 and 1903.

The Lilian Ward was named after Lilian Holland 1852 – 1896, the daughter of Stephen G. Holland and his wife Ann. According to the St. Thomas' Hospital Gazette:

> Stephen G. Holland Esq., a Governor of the Hospital defrayed all the expenses of the decorative work as a memorial to his daughter. The walls were tiled throughout with a series of charming picture panels, depicting nursery rhymes designed by Mr. W. Rowe, one of Messrs Doulton's Artists, who carried out the designs at their LAMBETH Works. At the opening ceremony Lord Lister said it was the most beautiful Children's Ward that ever existed.[23]

The panels, approximately 5 feet by 2 feet 6 inches, were set in the wall close together above a dado of plain tiles. They were arranged in sets, for example, three Dick Whittington scenes, two Jack and Jill and three Little Red Riding Hood etc., and there were twenty-five panels in all. The cost of the tiling was estimated at £655.12.6d.

(Detail from Puss in Boots)

Lilian Ward closed in the 1970s and fortunately the Special Trustees agreed to underwrite the sum of £28,000 for the removal of the panels and the cost of restoring and framing them for display in the new hospital. Trades Unions, the Victorian Society, the Doulton Collectors Club, local Societies and other bodies have contributed to the Doulton Tile Fund.

Seymour Ward was named after Seymour Graves Toller. The tile panels were also made by Doultons and were designed by William Rowe and Margaret Thompson, and were arranged in similar fashion to the panels in Lilian Ward. The detailed dedication inscription showed that the panels in the East and West Walls were *given by Lilian Jewesbury in ever loving memory of Seymour Graves Toller, M.D., M.R.C.P., late Physician to Kasr-el-Aini Hospital, Cairo, and late Physician to St. Thomas' Hospital.* Lilian Jewsbury was his fiancée. The panels on the South Wall were given by Allan Johnson Douglas of Montreal, and the North Wall panels by H.R.H. Ras Makonnen, K.C.M.G., Abyssinia, Crown Prince and Envoy of the Emperor to the Coronation of King Edward VII. His grandson, Haile Selassie, visited the hospital in later years.[24]

Seymour Ward was demolished and the panels were removed by the contractors. One panel, *The Babes in the Wood*, was given back to the hospital by Mr. Alistair MacAlpine and is now displayed in the Out Patients' Department. I have traced two of the Seymour Ward panels to an isolated farm in West Wales. They are the two *Puss in Boots* pictures. One of these has been bought by the Special Trustees of St. Thomas' Hospital to be restored and resited in the new Hospital.

LILIAN WARD.

1. *TURN AGAIN WHITTINGTON THRICE HONOURED CITIZEN*
2. *DICK WHITTINGTON ENTRUSTS HIS CAT TO THE CAPTAIN*
3. *DICK WHITTINGTON LORD MAYOR OF LONDON* (colour plate)
4. *JACK THE GIANT KILLER*
5. *JACK CLIMBS THE BEANSTALK*
6. *JACK ARRIVES AT THE GIANT'S CASTLE*
7. *JACK RUNS AWAY WITH THE GOLDEN HARP*
8. *JACK AND JILL WENT UP THE HILL TO FETCH A PAIL OF WATER*
9. *JACK FELL DOWN AND BROKE HIS CROWN AND JILL CAME TUMBLING AFTER*
10. *LITTLE MISS MUFFET SAT ON HER TUFFET EATING HER CURDS AND WHEY*
11. *GOODMORNING, RED RIDING HOOD SAID THE WOLF*
12. *RED RIDING HOOD PULLING THE BOBBINS TO OPEN THE DOOR*
13. *THE RESCUE OF RED RIDING HOOD AND DEATH OF THE WOLF*
14. *LITTLE BO-PEEP HAS LOST HER SHEEP*
15. *LET THEM ALONE AND THEY'LL COME HOME*
16. *CINDERELLA AND HER FAIRY GODMOTHER*
17. *CINDERELLA LEAVING THE BALL TWELVE O'CLOCK STRIKES*
18. *CINDERELLA TRIES ON THE GLASS SLIPPER*
19. *THE PRINCE AWAKES THE SLEEPING BEAUTY*
20. *LITTLE BOY BLUE COME BLOW UP YOUR HORN*
21 to 24. *SMALL PANELS OF TREES AND FLOWERS REPRESENTING THE SEASONS*

SEYMOUR WARD.

1. BABES IN THE WOOD. Now displayed in the Out Patients' Department.
2. PUSS IN BOOTS PRESENTS A RABBIT TO THE KING. (In a Welsh farmhouse).
3. PUSS IN BOOTS WATCHES THE KING'S GUARD PULL THE YOUNG MILLER FROM THE RIVER. (Returned to St. Thomas' from a Welsh farmhouse).

MISSING PANELS
HANSEL AND GRETEL. Two panels
LITTLE JACK HORNER. Two panels
THE GOOSE GIRL. Two panels
OLD KING COLE. Two panels
BABES IN THE WOOD. Second Panel

UNIVERSITY COLLEGE HOSPITAL, GOWER STREET, LONDON

NURSERY RHYMES AND FAIRY TALES, DOULTON

University College Hospital was mainly rebuilt between the years 1897 and 1905. Sir John Blundell Maple (Bart) is said to be the man responsible for providing the money. I was told that at one time there was an underground passageway leading from Maples Store to the Hospital to enable Maples' employees to have easy access for treatment.

In Ward 1, a former Children's Ward but now the Metabolic Ward, there were originally 24 tile pictures, several of which were signed by Margaret E. Thompson of Doulton. Extensive alterations were made when the ward change took place. Ceilings were lowered and office space created. This resulted in the obscuring of the tops of several of the pictures and some were completely covered over.

THE PICTURES.

1. THE SLEEPING BEAUTY 4 feet 6 inches × 3 feet
2. LITTLE RED RIDING HOOD 4 feet 6 inches × 3 feet
3. LITTLE RED RIDING HOOD AND THE WOLF 4 feet 6 inches × 3 feet
4. ORANGES AND LEMONS M.E. THOMPSON 4 feet 6 inches × 2 feet
5. JACK AND JILL WENT UP THE HILL 4 feet 6 inches × 3 feet
6. JACK FELL DOWN 4 feet 6 inches × 3 feet
7. OLD MOTHER HUBBARD 4 feet 6 inches × 2 feet
8. THERE WAS AN OLD WOMAN WHO LIVED IN A SHOE 4 feet 6 inches × 3 feet
9. HIGGLEDY PIGGLEDY MY BLACK HEN M.E. THOMPSON 4 feet 6 inches × 3 feet
10. SING A SONG OF SIXPENCE (Covered over) 4 feet 6 inches × 3 feet
11. SIMPLE SIMON WENT A FISHING (Covered over) 4 feet 6 inches × 3 feet
12. SEE SAW MARGERY DAW (Covered over) 4 feet 6 inches × 3 feet
13. LITTLE JACK HORNER 4 feet 6 inches × 2 feet
14. DING DONG BELL PUSSY'S IN THE WELL 4 feet 6 inches × 2 feet
15. LITTLE MISS MUFFET 4 feet 6 inches × 3 feet

16. LITTLE POLLY FLINDERS *M.E. THOMPSON* 4 feet 6 inches × 2 feet
17. HERE WE GO GATHERING NUTS IN MAY (Covered over) *M.E. THOMPSON* 4 feet 6 inches × 2 feet
18. JACK ESCAPES FROM THE GIANT'S CASTLE *M.E. THOMPSON* 4 feet 6 inches × 2 feet
19. CINDERELLA IN THE KITCHEN 4 feet 6 inches × 3 feet
20. LITTLE BO PEEP HAS LOST HER SHEEP
    4 feet 6 inches × 3 feet
21. MARY, MARY, QUITE CONTRARY This panel, no longer at the Hospital, was in the Doulton Exhibition at the Victoria and Albert Museum 1979, and is now in the Bethnal Green Museum.
22. LITTLE BO PEEP
23. GOOSEY GOOSEY GANDER
24. LADY QUEEN ANNE SHE SITS IN THE SUN

THE ROYAL WATERLOO HOSPITAL FOR CHILDREN AND WOMEN

NURSERY RHYMES AND FAIRY TALES – DOULTON

The Royal Waterloo Hospital Panels are now part of the St. Thomas' Hospital collection. The panels were in Helen Ward which, according to the St. Thomas' Hospital Gazette, was named after Her Royal Highness Helen Duchess of Albany, who laid the foundation stone of the hospital on 20 October 1903. The builders were Holliday and Greenwood, who gave some tile panels. Others were given by Messrs Charles Hunt and Bannister Smith, benefactors to the hospital, and one panel, *Rock-a-Bye Baby*, was presented by Mrs James Greenwood.

Five of the Royal Waterloo panels have been rescued and are now resited in St. Thomas' Hospital. There are two of *Little Red Riding Hood* and two of *Little Bo-Peep*. *Rock-a-Bye Baby* was cleaned and refurbished at the expense of an anonymous donor in memory of the late Norman Barrett, Consultant Surgeon to St. Thomas' Hospital.

Lilian, Seymour and Helen Wards now constitute the Children's Unit of the new St. Thomas Hospital.

ROYAL WATERLOO PICTURES NOW IN ST. THOMAS' HOSPITAL

HELEN WARD.

PANEL 1. *ROCK-A-BYE BABY. The gift of Mrs James Greenwood.*
PANEL 2. *LITTLE BO-PEEP HAS LOST HER SHEEP. The gift of Bannister Smith.*
PANEL 3. *LET THEM ALONE AND THEY'LL COME HOME. The gift of Mrs S. Holliday.*
PANEL 4. *RED RIDING HOOD MEETS THE WOLF. The gift of Charles Hunt.*
PANEL 5. *RED RIDING HOOD IN HER GRANDMOTHER'S COTTAGE. The gift of Mrs James Greenwood.*

THE FORMER WESTMINSTER HOSPITAL – MARIE CELESTE WARD

NURSERY RHYMES AND OTHER PICTURES – SIMPSON

An old sales leaflet of the tile firm W.B. Simpson and Sons lists Westminster Hospital as having been supplied with tiling. In March 1983 the part-time archivist of the Special Trustees of the Hospital told me that the Children's Ward, Marie Celeste, in Broad Sanctuary, demolished in 1952, was decorated with twelve tile pictures and that the *Nursing Mirror*[25] of 11 November 1933 contained a description and a photograph. Marie Celeste Ward was apparently a part of an extension added to the old Westminster Hospital in the mid 1920s.

The *Nursing Mirror* article had a picture of Westminster Hospital and one of the Children's Ward as it was in 1933, with the panels on the walls. The reporter gave a long account of her visit to the hospital in which she wrote:

> *our next visit was to the Marie Celeste Ward for children, where some little patients were sitting up having tea and others were playing in their cots. In this ward tiling and tile picture panels were provided from funds collected by Girl Guides and children from all parts of the British Empire.*

New information came to me in March 1985 from a viewer who had seen an item about my tile picture research on the *Blue Peter* BBC TV Programme. She sent me copies of pages from *The Guide*,[26] the weekly newspaper of the Girl Guides Association, from 1923, 1924, and 1925.

The story began when Mrs J. Young, Captain of the 1st Camberwell Company saw an appeal outside Westminster Hospital asking for contributions to the Fairy Tiles for the Children's Ward. She wrote to *The Guide* on 10 November 1923, suggesting that each Guide, Brownie and Guider from the London Companies might help and she had asked the Hospital Secretary to find out from the Architect how many tiles would be needed, and the cost of each one. By the following week she had learned that the cost of one tile would be approximately nine pence (9d = approximately 4p) and that about ten thousand were required.

On 26 January 1924 the Secretary of the Hospital, Charles M. Power, wrote to *The Guide* saying that he had been asked for information from Companies in many parts of the country. He said the Prince of Wales had promised to visit when the work was completed and he was anxious that the picture tiling would be finished by then. However, the tiling could not begin until he knew how much money he would get and he would like to know what the Companies might be able to contribute. He gave details of the estimated cost:

> *One tile costs 9 pence*
> *One small picture composed of 180 tiles £6.15 shillings*
> *One large picture composed of 693 tiles £26.0.0d.*
> *There will be at least two small pictures and several large pictures.*

On 9 February 1924 *The Guide* reproduced two of the proposed pictures, *Ride a Cock Horse* and *Mary had a Little Lamb*, so that the Companies should know what it was all about.

The Editor wrote to *My dear Guides* on 23 February saying that the hospital had mentioned the possibility of having something symbolic to show what the Guides had done. The Editor said, *I for one would like to see the Emblem of the Girl Guides side by side with the pictures for a perpetual reminder of what we can do for others.* By 1 March a list of fourteen Companies from as far apart as Truro, Finchley and Manchester had sent contributions and on 5 April twenty-six more were listed. The 20 September 1924 issue recorded £13 from nineteen Companies in Dorset. The issue of 21 March 1925 had a long letter from Mrs Young of the Camberwell Company who had started the appeal describing a visit to the hospital when she *saw the beautiful room with pale green and white tiles and coloured panels of fairy tales . . . which give much pleasure to the little ones lying in the beds: above the door, in brown letters, on the white tiles is this inscription.*

> THIS TABLET IS TO RECORD THE GENEROSITY
> OF THOSE MENTIONED HEREUNDER, WHO
> CONTRIBUTED TO THE PICTURE TILING OF
> THIS WARD

Heading the list were the Girl Guides and Brownies of the British Isles who had collected a total of £107.2s.1d. Apparently Mr Power wanted more money from the Guides and suggested that if they could raise £30 a year they could have a cot named after them.

The total cost of the pictures was in the region of £300, and they were probably similar to sets used in other hospitals such as Torbay in the same period. It is possible to identify the following from old photographs.

MARY HAD A LITTLE LAMB
RIDE A COCK HORSE
SING A SONG O SIXPENCE
GOOSEY GOOSEY GANDER
GATHERING FLOWERS
FEEDING THE POULTRY

What happened to the twelve panels when the ward was demolished? If they were destroyed in the demolition process so too was the visible record of voluntary effort and fund raising by the Girl Guide Movement and other people.

THE HOSPITAL FOR WOMEN, SOHO SQUARE, LONDON

DECORATIVE TILING – THE MEDMENHAM POTTERY CO.

In the entrance hall of the hospital stands a bust on which is inscribed –
PROTHEROE SMITH, FOUNDER FIRST HOSPITAL FOR WOMEN
He founded the original hospital for Diseases of Women in Red Lion Square and it was replaced by the Soho Square hospital in 1851. Opening a hospital to deal specifically with Diseases of Women was an outstanding advance in British medicine and gynaecology, but raising funds was difficult because in Victorian England the name suggested V.D., not a popular aim for subscribers, and the name was changed to The Hospital for Women. It is now a listed building.

A seven foot high area of tiling covers the lower part of the walls of the entrance hall. The background is an attractive pale grey, surrounded by a moulded frieze of two rows of 3 × 3 inch tiles, bordered above and below by a thin line of 1 × 3 inch tiles and broken at intervals by vertical lines of tiles 1 inch wide. On each side of the hall is a 12 × 12 inch panel with leaves, flowers and a dovelike bird.

The work is attributed to the Medmenham Pottery which was established as a rural industry in the 1890s at Marlow Common by Robert Hudson, of Sunlight Soap.[27] Recent research has produced a lot of new information about this little known pottery. Its London agent was William Höfler in Soho Square, where customers could view the range of tiles. It would be interesting to know whether the firm had any links with the hospital.

PRESTON HALL HOSPITAL, MAIDSTONE, KENT

PLAQUE – CARTER

In the Museum of the Poole Pottery Company there is a large (1 foot 6 inch × 1 foot) ceramic plaque containing the following words:

THE
EMPRESS CLUB
EMERGENCY VOLUNTARY AID COMMITTEE
35, DOVER STREET, LONDON, W.
GAVE THIS SHOP TO THE
PRESTON HALL COLONY
1923

Preston Hall was a large country house which became a home for the mentally handicapped and later a hospital for diseases of the chest.

THE ROYAL VICTORIA INFIRMARY, NEWCASTLE-UPON-TYNE

NURSERY RHYMES AND FAIRY TALES – DOULTON

During 1896 Mr. (later Sir) Riley Lord, the Mayor of Newcastle, suggested that a new Infirmary would be a fitting memorial for Queen Victoria's Diamond Jubilee. He began a public subscription aimed at raising £100,000. In 1897 a Mr John Hall offered another £100,000 on condition that it was matched by the public subscription. The foundation stone was laid on 20 June 1900 by H.R.H. the Prince of Wales. In 1901 Lord Armstrong of Cragside died and as a memorial to him, his heir W.A. Watson-Armstrong gave a further £100,000. The total sum of £300,000 was a very considerable amount of money and the hospital was subsequently opened by King Edward VII accompanied by Queen Alexandra on 11 July 1906. One of the architects was the well known Mr. Percy Adams.[28]

The first members of the public, the hospital staff, young patients and their relatives visiting the four Children's Wards could hardly have expected to see the remarkable display of tile pictures with many familiar and some less well known Nursery Rhymes and

Fairy Tales. There were probably sixty pictures at that time but ward alterations for storage and office space has reduced the number now on view to fifty five.

The pictures are in bright and attractive colours and eighty years later look as good as new. All were manufactured by Doulton at their Lambeth works in London and bear the signature or initials of three of Doulton's best known designers and artists:

W R – William Rowe

J H M L – J.H. McLennan

Margaret E. Thompson

It is always a bonus to discover who provided the money for the tile pictures in Children's Wards. A search through local newspaper files in Newcastle City Library revealed that the donors were:–

1. The Misses Stephenson, probably the daughters of the Lord Mayor of the time.
2. Mrs Albert Ward and her friends.
3. The Honorary Physicians and Surgeons.
4. The Workmen Governors.

On visits to the hospital I have found the pictures enthusiastically appreciated by patients, and nursing, medical and administrative staff. They have received a good deal of publicity and are used as illustrations for both the Nursery Rhymes and Fairy Tale Books published by Country Life Books in 1984 and 1985.

LADY BIRD LADY BIRD FLY AWAY HOME. WR & JHML 4 feet 6 inches × 2 feet

TOM TOM THE PIPERS SON STOLE THE PIG AND AWAY DID RUN. WR & JHML 4 feet 6 inches × 2 feet

TOM WENT ROARING DOWN THE STREET. WR & JHML 4 feet 6 inches × 2 feet

LITTLE GIRL LITTLE GIRL WHERE HAVE YOU BEEN. WR & JHML 4 feet 6 inches × 3 feet

LITTLE BO-PEEP HAS LOST HER SHEEP. WR & JHML 4 feet 6 inches × 2 feet

LET THEM ALONE AND THEY'LL COME HOME. WR & JHML 4 feet 6 inches × 2 feet

DING DONG BELL, PUSSY'S IN THE WELL. WR & JHML 4 feet 6 inches × 3 feet

LITTLE BETTY BLUE LOST HER HOLIDAY SHOE. M.E. THOMPSON 4 feet 6 inches × 2 feet

THERE WAS AN OLD WOMAN WHO LIVED IN A SHOE. M.E. THOMPSON 4 feet 6 inches × 3 feet

LITTLE TOMMY TUCKER SANG FOR HIS SUPPER. WR 4 feet 6 inches × 2 feet

CURLY LOCKS SHALL SEW A FINE SEAM AND FEED UPON STRAWBERRIES, SUGAR AND CREAM. JHML 4 feet 6 inches × 2 feet

HIGGLEDY PIGGLEDY, MY BLACK HEN. M.E. THOMPSON 4 feet 6 inches × 2 feet

LITTLE MISS MUFFET, SHE SAT ON A TUFFET. WR & JHML 4 feet 6 inches × 2 feet 6 inches

SIMPLE SIMON WENT A-FISHING. JHML 4 feet 6 inches × 3 feet

SIMPLE SIMON MET A PIEMAN. WR & JHML 4 feet 6 inches × 3 feet

HICKORY DICKORY DOCK, THE MOUSE RAN UP THE CLOCK. WR & JHML 4 feet 6 inches × 2 feet

THE CLOCK STRUCK ONE, THE MOUSE RAN DOWN. WR & JHML 4 feet 6 inches × 2 feet 3 inches

WHERE ARE YOU GOING MY PRETTY MAID? – I'M GOING A MILKING SIR SHE SAID. WR & JHML 4 feet 6 inches × 3 feet

THEN I CAN'T MARRY YOU MY PRETTY MAID – NOBODY ASKED YOU SIR, SHE SAID. WR & JHML 4 feet 6 inches × 3 feet

OLD MOTHER HUBBARD WENT TO THE CUPBOARD. M.E. THOMPSON 4 feet 6 inches × 2 feet

OLD MOTHER GOOSE. WR & JHML 4 feet 6 inches × 2 feet

THE KING WAS IN HIS COUNTING HOUSE, COUNTING OUT HIS MONEY. WR & JHML 4 feet 6 inches × 2 feet

THE MAID WAS IN THE GARDEN, HANGING OUT THE CLOTHES. WR & JHML 4 feet 6 inches × 2 feet

THE QUEEN WAS IN THE PARLOUR EATING BREAD AND HONEY. WR & JHML 4 feet 6 inches × 3 feet

I HAD A LITTLE HUSBAND. M.E. THOMPSON 4 feet 6 inches × 2 feet

PUSSY CAT, PUSSY CAT, WHERE HAVE YOU BEEN. M.E. THOMPSON 4 feet 6 inches × 2 feet

HUSH-A-BYE BABY, ON THE TREE TOP. WR & JHML 4 feet 6 inches × 2 feet

ST. SWITHIN'S DAY IF THOU DOST RAIN, FOR FORTY DAYS IT WILL REMAIN. M.E. THOMPSON 4 feet 6 inches × 3 feet (colour plate)

HERE WE GO FATHERING NUTS IN MAY. M.E. THOMPSON 4 feet 6 inches × 2 feet

LITTLE JACK HORNER SAT IN A CORNER M.E. THOMPSON 4 feet 6 inches × 2 feet

HUSH-A-BY BABY, ON THE TREE TOP. (VERSION TWO) M.E. THOMPSON 4 feet 6 inches × 2 feet

THE SLEEPING BEAUTY IN THE ENCHANTED PALACE. M.E. THOMPSON 4 feet 6 inches × 4 feet

Little Jack Horner
Sat in a corner

LITTLE BOY BLUE COME BLOW ON YOUR
HORN. WR & JHML 4 feet 6 inches × 2 feet
DAFFY-DOWN-DILLY HAS COME TO TOWN.
WR & JHML 3 feet 6 inches × 4 feet
HARK, HARK, THE DOGS DO BARK. M.E.
THOMPSON 3 feet 6 inches × 4 feet
OLD KING COLE WAS A MERRY OLD SOUL.
M.E. THOMPSON 3 feet 6 inches × 4 feet
BLOW WIND, BLOW, AND GO MILL GO. WR &
JHML 3 feet 6 inches × 4 feet
MARY, MARY QUITE CONTRARY, HOW
DOES YOUR GARDEN GROW. M.E.
THOMPSON 4 feet 6 inches × 2 feet
I HAVE BEEN UP TO LONDON TO SEE THE
QUEEN. WR & JHML 3 feet 6 inches × 4 feet
I SAW A SHIP A-SAILING. WR & JHML 3 feet 6
inches × 4 feet
BAA BAA, BLACK SHEEP, HAVE YOU ANY
WOOL? WR & JHML 4 feet 6 inches × 3 feet
GOOSEY-GOOSEY GANDER, WHITHER DOST
THOU WANDER? M.E. THOMPSON 4 feet 6
inches × 2 feet
LADY QUEEN ANNE SHE SITS IN THE SUN.
M.E. THOMPSON 4 feet 6 inches × 2 feet
OH, WHO IS SO MERRY, HEY HO! AS THE
LIGHT-HEARTED FAIRY, HEY HO! WR &
JHML 4 feet 6 inches × 2 feet
BLESS YOU, BLESS YOU BURNY BEE; SAY
WHEN WILL YOUR WEDDING BE? WR &
JHML 4 feet 6 inches × 2 feet
CINDERELLA IN THE CORNER. M.E.
THOMPSON 4 feet 6 inches × 2 feet
THE FAIRY SENDS CINDERELLA TO THE
BALL. M.E. THOMPSON 4 feet 6 inches × 3
feet
CINDERELLA PUTS ON THE GLASS SLIPPER.
M.E. THOMPSON 4 feet 6 inches × 2 feet
LUCY LOCKET LOST HER POCKET, KITTY
FISHER FOUND IT. M.E. THOMPSON 4 feet
6 inches × 3 feet
LITTLE RED RIDING HOOD. M.E. THOMPSON
4 feet 6 inches × 2 feet
THE KNAVE OF HEARTS WHO STOLE THE
TARTS. M.E. THOMPSON 4 feet 6 inches × 2
feet
MY MAID MARY, SHE MINDS THE DAIRY.
M.E. THOMPSON 4 feet 6 inches × 3 feet
AND JILL CAME TUMBLING AFTER. M.E.
THOMPSON 4 feet 6 inches × 2 feet
THE QUEEN OF HEARTS SHE MADE SOME
TARTS. M.E. THOMPSON 4 feet 6 inches × 2
feet 6 inches

My maid Mary,
She minds the Dairy.

ST. NICHOLAS HOSPITAL, GOSFORTH, NEWCASTLE-UPON-TYNE

TILED PROSCENIUM ARCH OF RECREATION HALL STAGE – DOULTON

The building containing the Recreation Hall of St. Nicholas Hospital was opened on 30 May 1900, according to a plaque in the main entrance bearing the names of Sir W.H. Stephenson, J.P., Chairman of the Visiting Committee; J.T. Calcott, Medical Superintendent; Riley Lord (later Sir), Mayor and J.T. Forster, Sheriff. A Mr Walter Scott was the Contractor.

The stage is 16 feet high and 21 feet wide and is surrounded by an Art Nouveau scheme of highly decorative Doulton tiling, made up of 6 × 6 inch tube lined polychrome tiles showing beautiful birds, flowers, and trees surrounded by two Pre-Raphaelite ladies in flowing garments. The plainer areas consist of 9 × 12 inch faience slabs. (Detail – colour plate)

The scheme, the only one of its kind in any hospital, is a rare find in a mental hospital of that date. The designer was W.J. Neatby, an architect by profession who worked as an artist and designer for Doultons in Lambeth from 1890 until 1907. His best known works include the decorative tiling of Harrods Food Hall, the Everard building in Bristol and the interior of Blackpool Tower.[29]

The choice of a Doulton tiling scheme may have been connected with a Doulton tiling plan for Newcastle Royal Infirmary around the same time. The leading personalities of St. Nicholas Hospital were also prominent in the Royal Infirmary fund raising.

WHITLINGHAM HOSPITAL, TROWSE, NORWICH

DELFT AND OTHER TILING – MAKERS UNKNOWN

Whitlingham Hospital is partly housed in a mid-Victorian Country House dating from circa 1860 but largely refurbished in 1905.
   Description of tiling:–
1.   Three of the toilets are tiled to a height of five feet in plain green 5 inch tiles. In one of the toilets a lavatory bowl has the date 1892. The door furniture is designed in the Arts and Crafts Movement style.
2.   Two tiled fireplaces in the Nurses' Home would appear to be of the same period – 1892.
3.   In the original servants' side of the house there is a five foot dado of plain cream tiles with a green glint, finished off with black moulded tiles.
4.   In the kitchen there are blue and white tiles forming a geometric design.
5.   In the original nursery on the top floor are blue and white Delft tiles of unknown date.

BRANDRETH HOSPITAL, ORMSKIRK, LANCASHIRE

A FRIEZE OF CHILDREN AND ANIMALS – MAW

The hospital is named after its founder, Dr. Joseph Brandreth. It was first known as the Brandreth Dispensary and later as the Cottage Hospital, which was opened by the Countess of Derby on 22 January 1896.

In a former Children's Ward there is a frieze of picture tiles above a green tiled dado, running all round the ward. The picture tiling consists of a row of two 6 × 6 inch tiles, bordered above by a row of 6 × 2 inch green glazed tiles.

1. HENS, COWS AND A CALF WITH A HOUSE IN THE BACKGROUND.
2. TIGER AND CUBS.
3. ELEPHANT AND CALF.
4. LION AND LIONESS.
5. CHILD ON A DONKEY AND OTHER CHILDREN PLAYING ON THE SEASHORE.
6. DUTCH CHILDREN AND DUTCH ADULTS WITH GEESE AND HENS.
7. CHILDREN SWIMMING IN A RIVER AND BOY AND GIRL EATING APPLES.
8. BOY AND GIRL ON SCOOTERS.
9. BOY AND GIRL FEEDING A CAT.
10. CHILDREN RIDING ON TOY ANIMALS.
11. CHILDREN PICKING APPLES.
12. CHILDREN SKATING ON ICE.
13. BOY WITH A WHIP AND OTHER CHILDREN AT PLAY.

A similar frieze of picture tiles in Heswall Hospital, in the Wirral, has been identified as the work of Maws, Jackfield, Shropshire. An elderly former employee of Maws has some recollection of having painted the pictures when working under the direction of Edward W. Ball, the artist whose signed pictures occur in St. Hilda's, Hartlepool and Bronglais Hospital, Aberystwyth.

THE RADCLIFFE INFIRMARY, OXFORD

FLOORS – MINTON

A note in *The Builder* on 5 December 1863 is the only information I have on the Radcliffe Infirmary but I have included it because it seems a most unusual use of tiles in a hospital.

The spaces on the floor under each bed are covered with white glazed Minton tiles with a glazed red border. These tiles were bedded in Portland cement which rests on a bed of concrete laid between the joists. Any moisture therefore spilt under the bed will be upon the tiles and may easily be wiped off the polished surface. Between the bed spaces the floor is as elsewhere, of wainscot, the tiles not projecting beyond the edge of an ordinary bed that they may not be stepped on by patients leaving their beds.[30]

POOLE DISTRICT GENERAL HOSPITAL, POOLE, DORSET.

DECORATIVE TILING IN ENTRANCE – CARTER / PILKINGTON

Poole District Hospital was built in the 1970s and is one of the few constructed in recent years to have tiles as a decorative feature. The tiling was manufactured at the nearby Pilkington factory which was formerly known as Carters.

One wall of the Main Entrance corridor is lined with off-white tiles forming a background to a pleasantly designed series of pictures of stylised flowers in attractive shades of brown. The scheme is in marked contrast to the bare walls of entrance halls and corridors in so many of our modern hospitals.

THE ROYAL PORTSMOUTH HOSPITAL

THREE RELIGIOUS, TWO NURSERY RHYMES AND ONE FAIRY TALE – DOULTON

When the Royal Portsmouth Hospital was closed in 1979 and was due for demolition, the City Council decided to have the tile panels removed, restored and re-sited in the City Museum. The work was undertaken by the staff of the Ironbridge Gorge Museum where visitors to the Tile Department were able to see the delicate work of restoration being done using modern techniques.

The panels were put in the Children's Ward in 1908 when it changed from being a Fever Ward. Two are signed by William Rowe. One panel, *A little child shall lead them*, commemorates the raising of £3,000 for the endowment of two cots by the Mayor and Mayoress of Portsmouth. The Mayoress was a little girl of only five years old, her father being a widower. She is said to have *performed her part with charming success* and raised more than £1,000 which was spent on the tile pictures.[31]

The Nursery Rhyme and Fairy Tale panels, 6 feet 6 inches × 3 feet although bearing dedication dates of 1932 are in the style of earlier Doulton work and are believed to have been also designed by William Rowe.

1. *A LITTLE CHILD SHALL LEAD THEM. To commemorate the raising of £1,000 for the endowment of two cots by Mr. F.G. Foster and Miss Doris Foster, Mayor and Mayoress of Portsmouth, 1907 – 1908.*
2. *AND THEY BROUGHT UNTO HIM LITTLE CHILDREN. Presented by Portsmouth and District Sunday School Children.*
3. *THE COMING OF THE CHRIST CHILD. Presented by the Gosport Sunday School Union in memory of Benjamin Nicholson Esq., J.P. who was for 56 years the Honorary Secretary of the Union.*
4. *THERE WAS AN OLD WOMAN WHO LIVED IN A SHOE. Presented to the Portsmouth Royal Hospital as a Souvenir of Miss Florence Jane White and her work for children.*
5. *THE QUEEN OF HEARTS. Presented by the Staff and Students of the Portsmouth Training College as a Souvenir of Miss E.L. White, M.A. Principal 1907 – 1932.*
6. *LITTLE RED RIDING HOOD. Presented by the Staff and Students of the Portsmouth Training College as a Souvenir of Miss E.L. White, M.A. Principal 1907 – 1932.*

PRESTON ROYAL INFIRMARY, LANCASHIRE

NURSERY RHYMES AND FAIRY TALES – MAKER UNKNOWN
DOMESTIC ANIMALS AND BIRDS – MAKER UNKNOWN

The Alderman Thomas Parkinson Children's Ward in the Princess Mary Wing of the Hospital and the adjoining single rooms date from 1929 to 1935.

A new hospital is being built and the hospital staff are hopeful that the tiling can be rescued and resited in the new Children's Ward. The tile panels, all 4 feet × 2 feet 6 inches, are quite different from all others I have seen and there is no evidence of the manufacturer or the artist who designed and painted them. They are all of excellent quality, some have a flat glazed surface and others are tube lined. Two nursery rhyme pictures are particularly interesting in that they show Little Bo-Peep searching for her sheep, and Cinderella leaving the ball at midnight, in the style of dress associated with the 1920s.

The animal and bird pictures are on individual six inch tiles set amongst plain tiling in the side wards and offices. They are also unmarked but are similar to some I have since seen in the Derbyshire Children's Hospital.

1. JACK AND JILL.
2. LITTLE MISS MUFFET.
3. LITTLE JACK HORNER.
4. OLD MOTHER HUBBARD.
5. LITTLE BOY BLUE. (colour plate)
6. OLD WOMAN WHO LIVED IN A SHOE.
7. LITTLE BO-PEEP.
8. PUSS IN BOOTS.
9. RED RIDING HOOD.
10. DICK WHITTINGTON.
11. CINDERELLA.
12. JACK AND THE BEANSTALK.

INDIVIDUAL PICTURE TILES – 6 × 6 inches

SQUIRREL.
TWO GEESE.
DOG.
DUCKLING.
OWL.
RABBIT.
HARE.
COCKEREL.
SWAN.
WILD DUCK.
PET RABBIT.
FROG.

Each tile is repeated several times.

BOROCOURT HOSPITAL, WYFOLD, NEAR READING, BERKS.

RELIGIOUS SCENE – GIBBS AND HOWARD
FLOORS AND FIREPLACES – MINTON

Borocourt Hospital was opened in 1932 in the former Wyfold Court. The hospital acquired its name from the initial letters of the four local authorities, Buckinghamshire, Oxfordshire, Reading, and Oxford, and provided accommodation for mentally handicapped patients from those areas.[32]

Wyfold Court has been described as the major work of a little known architect, George Somers Clarke the elder, and it was said to be the grandest and most elaborate house in the country built in the French late Gothic style. It was built during the 1870s for Edward Hermon, a member of the firm of Horrocks, Miller and Co., Cotton Spinners of Preston in Lancashire, while he was representing that town as Member of Parliament from 1868 to 1881. The mansion is now the Administration Centre for this large hospital and its 264 acres of parkland provides space for occupation, recreation, and social activities for the patients.

1. TILED CORRIDORS. These are floored with black and white tiles forming a geometric pattern bordered by black tiles and a narrower border line of tiling.
2. GOTHIC FIREPLACE IN LIBRARY. Decorated tiles.
    GOTHIC FIREPLACE IN DRAWING ROOM. Decorated tiles.
    GOTHIC FIREPLACE IN BALLROOM. Decorated tiles.
3. LARGE TILE PICTURE. A gilt framed tile picture is set against the main corridor wall and shows a religious allegorical scene with Christ in an attitude of blessing and preaching to people. A Latin text surrounds the whole picture and is roughly translated as *Whatever the people order, justice does the same, that which the greater part decrees, the same do justice reason.*

    The picture bears the name: *I.A. Gibbs & Howard, 64, Charlotte Street, Fitzroy Square, London*, a firm known as stained glass painters and responsible for mosaic pictures in Victorian churches.

THE ROYAL BERKSHIRE HOSPITAL, LONDON ROAD, READING

NURSERY RHYMES, FAIRY TALES AND DOMESTIC SCENES – SIMPSON

It took me a long time to track down the tiles in the Royal Berkshire Hospital. Several enquiries produced negative results until two members of the Tile Society gave me useful information. One had recollections of seeing Nursery Rhyme pictures while training at the hospital many years ago, and the second happened to visit a friend who was ill and confirmed their existence.

I visited the hospital in November 1983 and was delighted to find a fine series of tile pictures in the King Edward VII Ward. I was told that the building dated from 1911 and this fitted in with the style of a series of W.B. Simpson and Sons' pictures in the 1912 Boscombe Hospital.

14 PANELS – MOSTLY 6 × 3 feet.

1. *LITTLE BOY BLUE*
2. *DICK WHITTINGTON*
3. *PUSS IN BOOTS*
4. *BRINGING HOME THE MILK*
5. *BRINGING HOME THE SHEEP*
6. *JACK AND THE BEANSTALK*
7. *RIDE A COCK HORSE*
8. *GOOSEY GOOSEY GANDER*
9. *LITTLE BO-PEEP*
10. *GOODY TWO SHOES*
11. *MARY HAD A LITTLE LAMB* – partly obscured
12. *BUTTERCUPS AND DAISIES*
13. Totally obscured
14. A 5 × 4 feet picture of the Royal Coat of Arms and the lettering *KING EDWARD VII WARD* framed by leafy scrolls with the Thistle, Shamrock and English Rose. (colour plate)

SHREWSBURY EYE AND E.N.T. HOSPITAL, SHREWSBURY

TILE PICTURES – MAW

Shrewsbury Eye and Ear, Nose and Throat Hospital dates from 1881. The architect was C.R. Ellison. It is an attractive red brick building with some excellent external terracotta figures and architectural features said to be the work of the Tiles and Terracotta Manufacturers J.C. Edwards, Ruabon, Wales.

In the hospital entrance and below a tall staircase window are three tile panels representing Faith, Hope and Charity. The figures were originally for a church reredos by a Mr Weatherstone and were considerably modified by Charles Henry Temple (1857 – 1940) who actually painted them. Temple worked as an artist for Maws from 1887 to 1906 and has been described as their best and most influential designer.

A frame of heavily moulded six inch tiles surrounds the pictures, each of which is made up of 12 six inch tiles.

1. FAITH. A female figure in pre-Raphaelite dress holding what appears to be a light.
2. CHARITY. A female figure in the attitude of giving.
3. HOPE. A female figure holding a book and with the other hand held high.

STAMFORD AND RUTLAND HOSPITAL, STAMFORD, LINCOLNSHIRE

AGRICULTURAL AND SEASONAL ACTIVITIES – MAKER UNKNOWN ? MINTON

Stamford Infirmary was built in 1828 more on the lines of a country house than a hospital. The Marquess of Exeter from nearby Burghley was the first Chairman of its Committee and his successors remained closely associated with the hospital until recent times. It had very

strict rules and several common illnesses were excluded, and Cholera patients in 1832 were not allowed anywhere near this hospital.[33] Extensions were added in 1842, and in 1879 three blocks were built to accommodate patients suffering from infectious diseases in order to comply with the Public Health Act of 1875.

The tile pictures probably date from that period but there is no evidence why such good examples of ceramic decoration were chosen. They are distinctive and of high quality. Five pictures each measuring three feet by two feet in sepia and a pale blueish-grey depict men and women engaged in agricultural activities such as harvesting, apple picking and ploughing. Two large polychrome panels in the style of the ceramic artist Albert Slater show people skating in a winter scene; and a ploughman and horses in a rural setting. The latter has been partly obscured by a cupboard fitted to the wall.

For a time some of the pictures were painted over but fortunately the appreciative hospital staff have had them cleaned and are justly proud of them.

1. WINTER SCENE WITH SHEPHERD, A RIVER IN THE BACKGROUND. 3 × 2 feet
2. MEN PLOUGHING WITH A PAIR OF HORSES. 3 × 2 feet
3. TWO MEN AND A WOMAN APPLE PICKING. 3 × 2 feet
4. TWO MEN AND A WOMAN SCYTHING HAY. 3 × 2 feet
5. THREE MEN AND A WOMAN REAPING CORN. 3 × 2 feet
6. WINTER SKATING SCENE. POLYCHROME. 3 × 2 feet
7. RURAL SCENE, WITH HORSES AND A MAN PLOUGHING IN THE DISTANCE. POLYCHROME. 5 feet 6 inches × 2 feet 6 inches

STOCKPORT INFIRMARY, THE METROPOLITAN BOROUGH OF STOCKPORT

FOUR NURSERY RHYME TILE PANELS – P. O'BRIEN

Stockport Infirmary dates from 1833 but has been extensively added to in subsequent years.

The tile pictures are in Sykes Ward which was built as a Children's Ward in 1921 – 1922. The name Sykes was associated with the Infirmary from its early days and members of the family have held offices as President, Chairman and Treasurer of the Hospital Committee.

The tile pictures date from 1958 and are signed by an artist named Peter O'Brien. I have been unable to trace either the artist or the makers of the tiles and it is very unusual to find tile pictures being made and sited in hospitals at this date. The four panels, each made up of sixteen 6 × 6 inch tiles with 6 × 3 inch borders, are hand painted in life like colours with iridescent water in the spilling pail, the cockle shells, and the silver bells.

In the ward entrance is a commemorative plaque which states that the tile pictures were given to the Ward by Sister Bruce on her retirement as Sister of the Children's Ward.

Enquiries at the hospital and Stockport Library have produced no further information.

Nursery rhymes painted in a clear modern style, with lettering of the verse surrounding each picture.

1. *HEY DIDDLE DIDDLE THE CAT AND THE FIDDLE,*
   THE COW JUMPED OVER THE MOON,
   THE LITTLE DOG LAUGHED TO SEE SUCH FUN,
   AND THE DISH RAN AWAY WITH THE SPOON.
2. *JACK AND JILL WENT UP THE HILL,*
   TO FETCH A PAIL OF WATER,
   JACK FELL DOWN AND BROKE HIS CROWN,
   AND JILL CAME TUMBLING AFTER.
3. *HUMPTY DUMPTY SAT ON A WALL,*
   HUMPTY DUMPTY HAD A GREAT FALL,
   ALL THE KINGS HORSES AND ALL THE KINGS MEN,
   COULDN'T PUT HUMPTY TOGETHER AGAIN.
4. *MARY MARY QUITE CONTRARY,*
   HOW DOES YOUR GARDEN GROW,
   WITH SILVER BELLS AND COCKLE SHELLS,
   AND PRETTY MAIDS ALL IN A ROW.

LONGTON HOSPITAL, LONGTON, STOKE-ON-TRENT

PLAQUE – MAKER UNKNOWN

Longton Hospital dates from the 1920s. It is included only to show an example of the use of ceramic tiling as a memorial plaque which measures four feet by three feet and is made up of forty-eight tiles.

Longton was one of the many areas of tile manufacturing in Staffordshire and the tiled plaque reads:–

1914   THIS TABLET COMMEMORATES   1918
THE GIFT OF £1000
TOWARDS THIS BUILDING AS A
WAR MEMORIAL OFFERING
FROM THE
LONGTON MANUFACTURERS

NORTH STAFFORDSHIRE ROYAL INFIRMARY, STOKE-ON-TRENT

FLORAL DESIGNS – UNIDENTIFIED
ART NOUVEAU – CORN BROS.

North Staffordshire Royal Infirmary has been in existence for over one hundred years. At the entrance to Victoria Children's Ward there is a dedication plaque in white tiling with black lettering and it measures approximately twenty inches by twelve inches. It says that the Ward was donated in 1882 for the Surgical diseases of women. In recent years it became a Children's Ward.

There are 12 unusual and attractive pictures each made up of fifteen six inch tiles, showing hanging baskets of flowers, foliage and ribbons in light brown, green, blue and pale pink. Four feet from the ground is a floral dado made up of running sprays of moulded tiling of blue flowers, pink roses and foliage. The window bays have vertical panels of roses, blue flowers and sprays of green foliage.

The entrance hall of the hospital has an impressive area of tiling in Art Nouveau style. There are eight floral designs on each wall framed in green and a large border at the top of the walls consists of swags in green, yellow and blue.

On the left hand wall is a six inch tile carrying the following dedication:–

THE TILING OF THIS HALL WAS GIVEN
BY THE EMPLOYEES OF BULLERS LIMITED.

The makers of the entrance hall tiles were Corn Bros, a Staffordshire firm, well known for Art Nouveau work at the turn of the century.

TORBAY HOSPITAL, TORQUAY

NURSERY RHYMES AND DOMESTIC ACTIVITIES – SIMPSON

On 25 June 1925, Mrs Ella Rowcroft, a member of the Wills Tobacco family, wrote to the President of the Torbay Hospital Committee with an offer of £100,000 for the building of a new hospital. The architects were Adams, Holden and Pearson with H. Percy Adams named as the consultant architect. Mrs Rowcroft laid the foundation stone on 23 June 1926 and the opening ceremony was performed by Lord Mildmay of Flete on 17 November 1928.[34]

Long before I became interested in the subject I recall seeing the tile panels in Louisa Cary Children's Ward when I was a member of the Hospital Management Committee. Identification of the manufacturers proved difficult until 1983 when I met Mr Lionel Simpson, a retired member of the Simpson Tile Firm, who told me that he had negotiated the contract with the architects. Mr Percy Adams proposed that the tile pictures be used and his firm gave four of the panels. He specified that *each would measure 2 feet 6 inches × 4 feet 6 inches and altogether there would be twenty-one of them. Around each would be a green and white surround whilst below would be a dado of green tiles and above white tiles extending to the ceiling.* Two artists' sketches of the tile pictures have recently been discovered at Torbay Hospital. Mr Simpson thinks the artist was Mr Watt or a Mr Gurry. In addition to the architects, other donors of tile pictures included the builder, Mr. Burgess of London and his daughter, the Nursing Staff, the Trades and Labour Council, local schools and firms and private persons.

1. *JACK AND THE BEANSTALK*
2. *GOOSEY GOOSEY GANDER*
3. *CINDERELLA*
4. *LITTLE MISS MUFFET*
5. *LITTLE BOY BLUE*
6. *MARY HAD A LITTLE LAMB*
7. *GLEANING*
8. *FEEDING THE POULTRY*
9. *BUTTERCUPS AND DAISIES*
10. *DICK WHITTINGTON*
11. *LITTLE JACK HORNER*
12. *RIDE A COCK HORSE*
13. *THE BABES IN THE WOOD*
14. *THE GOOSE THAT LAID THE GOLDEN EGG*
15. *THE OLD WOMAN WHO LIVED IN A SHOE*
16. *CHANGING PASTURES*
17. *GOODY TWO SHOES*
18. *LITTLE BO-PEEP*
19. *WHERE ARE YOU GOING MY PRETTY MAID?*
20. *SING A SONG OF SIXPENCE*
21. *THE GOLDEN GOOSE*

A new District Hospital has now been built in the grounds of Torbay Hospital. In the main entrance of the Out Patients' Department there is a ceramic mural covering one of the walls. It lends brightness and colour and must provide a focus of interest and conversation for the thousands of people who enter the hospital. The Hospital Authorities have provided the following explanation for the benefit of patients and visitors.

TREE OF LIFE

A mosaic mural by Arthur Goodwin

The design of the mural is based on a simple tree form. The tree is an image which occurs frequently in legend and mythology as a symbol of life. In the centre lower part of the design are the roots and the earth, while the upper part signifies the abundance of life with its varied forms and colours, and contains indications of life's continuance into the future (eggs, seeds, fruits). The trunk is composed of two interlocking spirals which are derived from the DNA molecule, a basic structural unit of living matter. These spirals are echoed by the spirals of the two snakes in the old emblem for medicine represented on the left. Thus the ancient arts of healing are related to modern discoveries of science.

The background to the tree recalls the environment of Torbay with its complex of urban and rural communities in close relationship with the sea. The coat of arms with its apt motto, SALUS ET FELICITAS, Health and Happiness, makes a further reference to the locality.

At the base and to left and right are the alchemic symbols for the four elements, Fire, Water, Air and Earth. In the bottom centre are suggestions of past life in fossils (also a reference to the richness of local geology) and remote forms in the depth of the sea. Framing the lower sides are old symbols for the four seasons set in appropriate colours.

The tree grows between the Sun and Moon which are also symbols for male and female, and indications of the rhythmic flow of life between day and night. The bird is the future, its wings the power of life to transcend material limitations. Lines of the mosaic tesserae circling the Moon and Sun harmonize with the lines of the tree, and continuing into the sky might suggest the yet unknown tracks of life through distant space.

THE FORMER TUNBRIDGE WELLS GENERAL HOSPITAL

NURSERY RHYMES AND FAIRY TALES – SIMPSON
(NOW LOST)

Queen Victoria's Diamond Jubilee in 1897 provided an ideal opportunity for public spirited people in Tunbridge Wells to commemorate the event by proposing that the Jubilee Fund of £3,000 be used for a separate Children's Hospital. Outbreaks of scarlet fever had caused the Children's Ward of the General Hospital to close twice during the year 1896.

In 1899 it was agreed that what was really needed was a much larger scheme which would provide more General Wards as well as a special ward for children. In 1901 Mr Percy Adams was chosen as architect and he estimated the cost as £20,000. Work started in October 1902 when the cheapest tender of £21,983 was accepted. The new children's ward was opened for patients in August 1904 and the tiling was fully described:

> *Dark green tiles rise to a height of five feet around the walls. Above this, between each window, is a picture panel on tiles by Artists to represent familiar Nursery Rhymes and Children's Stories. Each has been given by a kind donor, and the idea which has resulted in such pretty effect is in imitation of that which has been widely adopted elsewhere.*[35]

The panels represent a variety of subjects.

1. *GOOSEY GOOSEY GANDER* Presented by Mr. C.R. Fletcher Lutwidge.
2. *SING A SONG O SIXPENCE* Presented by the Masonic brethren of the Homesdale Lodge.
3. *PUSS IN BOOTS* Presented by Reginald Neville Stone.
4. *BUTTERCUPS AND DAISIES* Presented by Miss S.E. Berry in memory of G.A. Berry M.B.
5. *JACK AND THE BEANSTALK* Presented by H.R. Knipe.
6. *LITTLE BOY BLUE* Presented by Mrs E. Elvy Robb Mayoress 1903–04.
7. *LITTLE GOODY TWO SHOES* Presented by R. Benson Jowitt.
8. *WHERE ARE YOU GOING MY PRETTY MAID?* Presented by Alex R. Cheare.
9. *LITTLE JACK HORNER* Presented by John Webster.
10. *LITTLE BO PEEP* Presented by Dr. R.T. Piggott.
11. *DICK WHITTINGTON* Presented by the Masonic Brethren of Pantiles Lodge.
12. *THE BABES IN THE WOOD* Mr. C.F. Gooch.
13. *MARY HAD A LITTLE LAMB* Mrs. Julius C. Drew.
14. *RIDE A COCK HORSE* Presented in gratitude by the very poor.
15. *THE GOLDEN GOOSE* Mr. C.R.F. Lutwidge.
16. *CINDERELLA* Canon and Mrs Scott in Memoriam.

The panel given by the very poor is significant of the gratitude felt by those who have benefitted from the work of the Hospital. The necessary sum was collected in pence and a very occasional piece of silver.

All the foregoing information is quoted from research by Carolyn Wraight of Tunbridge Wells, a member of the Tiles and Architectural Ceramic Society. I have been able to identify the tile pictures from a contemporary photograph which she found.

The hospital building was sold and demolished in 1935 and nothing is so far known of what became of the tile pictures.

KENT AND SUSSEX HOSPITAL, TUNBRIDGE WELLS, KENT

NURSERY RHYMES AND LITTLE ANIMALS – CARTER

The Kent and Sussex Hospital foundation stone was laid by the Duchess of York in 1932 and the building was completed in 1934 and opened by the Marchioness Camden C.B.E. The dedication stone recording the transfer of the hospital from voluntary to state control in 1949 was placed in the entrance hall by *The Fourth Marquis of Abergavenny and the Fifth Marchioness Camden to mark the association of their families with the hospital from its beginning and to remember 120 years devoted service to the sick by the men and women of this place.*

In the *Carter Picture Tiles for Hospitals* advertising booklet in the 1930s a reference is made to a scheme of tiling at Tunbridge Wells for a children's ward.[36] In the history of the Poole Pottery Company Jennifer Hawkins mentioned the order but said the scheme was used instead at another hospital.[37]

As a result of a conversation with a former member of staff I visited the hospital in September 1982. In a side ward I found three Nursery Rhyme panels and in the main ward I was shown the outline of a frieze of picture tiling covered by sections of hardboard. Some older members of staff had vague memories of the tiling but it seemed that this was the scheme that Carter's catalogue referred to. By keeping in touch with the hospital administrator I got an assurance that the tiles would be uncovered again. In September 1985 I was very glad to hear that the pictures had been revealed, to the delight of the ward staff and adult patients, the main ward being no longer used for children.

Carolyn Wraight of the Tiles and Architectural Ceramics Society kindly did some research for me and produced the following extract from the *Kent and Sussex Courier Peanut Club Page.*

20 July 1934. Aunt Agatha's Page. *Gifts and donations may be brought to the Peanut Shop and I hope . . . a great many half crowns for Nursery Tiles. I only wish we had all our Nursery Tile money . . . we need a lot more half crowns to reach the £1,000 we set ourselves to provide.*

27 July 1934. *Wonderful news for our Nursery Tile Fund: the first of all our beautiful tiles are really up and fixed in the Children's Ward. The cost of £200 for them all is more than anticipated.*

10 August 1934. *Ever since the opening of our new hospital when hundreds of people went through the Peanut Ward and saw those beautiful tiles looking so fresh and gay, we have had a steady stream of half crowns coming in from Good Friends all over the place.*

Up to the present we have just cleared £110 toward the £200 for our payment for the tiles.

Half a crown pays for one complete tile and the name of the donor will be entered in a handsome leather bound book.

Now that the tiles are really up I can give you full details about the various panels . . .

At the entrance of the Ward is the big Noah's Ark, the biggest panel of all, and very lovely it is too with its fresh colouring. This has cost £25.0.0. (5 feet 6 inches × 3 feet 6 inches) [colour plate]

Then there are six panels with animals on each costing £9.0.0. (4 feet 9 inches × 1 foot 6 inches)

Twelve Panels each costing £8.0.0. (4 feet 3 inches × 1 foot 6 inches)

Twelve Panels each costing £8.0.0. (4 feet 3 inches × 1 foot 6 inches)

Two Panels each costing £6.10.0. (3 feet 9 inches × 1 foot 6 inches)

Two small Panels at £6.0.0 each. (3 feet 3 inches × 1 foot 6 inches)

So far we have had two complete panels given us. The Kent VAD 74 have provided one of the eight panels, and one of the small panels with Paddy Fox and Beaver on it has been given by the High Broom Infants School.

We've still a long way to go to reach the £200.

12 October Peanut Club. Every week brings in a few more half crowns for our Nursery Tile Fund ... we still need £59.15s. for the beautifully hand painted tiles.

THE SIDE WARD PANELS

Panel 1. TOM, TOM, THE PIPER'S SON. 3 feet 6 inches × 2 feet 6 inches

Panel 2. MARY MARY QUITE CONTRARY. 3 feet 6 inches × 2 feet 6 inches

Panel 3. LITTLE BOY BLUE. 3 feet 6 inches × 2 feet 6 inches

(Detail from Mary Mary Quite Contrary)

WEST KIRBY RESIDENTIAL SCHOOL, THE WIRRAL

UNUSUAL TILE PICTURES OF CHILDREN AND ANIMALS – DOULTON

West Kirby Residential School celebrated its centenary in 1981. Its archives were listed by the Health Records Survey Team from Liverpool University in 1981.[38] I was not aware of this when I visited in July 1982 and recorded thirty-four Doulton tile pictures ranging in date from 1889 to the 1950s. The school was originally a convalescent home for children.

List of Tile Pictures:–

1. In Room 32. Tile picture by *Doulton and Co.* A garden scene with children, a baby, and a cat. Date 1889. 6 × 2 feet

2. In Staff Lounge Room 30. Tile picture similar in style to the above with a view of children in an apple orchard, signed *A. Dennis.*

62

Ada Dennis worked at Doulton's Lambeth Pottery from 1881 to 1894. 6 × 2 feet.

The following tile panels are of a type unique to this building with oval borders enclosing groups of children, painted in a delicate and distinctive style, with small clear lettering.

3. In the Girl's Lounge, Room 36, Ground Floor. Ten tile pictures painted on six 6 × 6 inch tiles and set in the wall. The pictures record the endowment of children's cots and all are manufactured by Doulton and Co. Lambeth.

The *Rippenden and District Nursing Association Cot AD 1948. Marked with acknowledgement to H. Willibeek Le Mair, Doulton and Co., Lambeth.*
Two children watching a boy rolling pastry.

The *Matron's Cot. Miss G.C. Fellows. Endowed by Peter Brown.*
Five children in a winter scene.

Cot in memory of Harris and Claude Tomkinson 1931.
Children in a summer scene.

The *Frank White Cot endowed by his wife and son John 1943.*
Oranges and Lemons.

The *Robert and Beatrice Rowland Cot. A D 1944.*
Pussy Cat where have you been?

The *Walter Harding Cot. Endowed by Nursing Staff 1941.*
Children by the sea side.

The *Julia Rae Cot endowed by her daughter Alice Rae.*
Hush-a-Bye-Baby on the tree top.

In memory of Mary Elizabeth Nickson and Ethel May Green her daughter 1943. Doulton Lambeth S.E.1. with acknowledgements to H. Willibeek Le Mair and David McKay Co. U.S.A.
Mother reading to her children.

The *George Rae Cot endowed in memory of George Rae, Red Court, Birkenhead, by his daughter Alice Rae October 11 Anno Dom 1903.*
Mary Mary quite contrary. (colour plate)

The *Alice Rae Cot endowed in loving memory of Alice of Red Court, Birkenhead, by her nieces and nephews 1939.*
Baa Baa Black Sheep.

4. In an upstairs Girl's Dormitory. Eight Tile Pictures all 1 foot 6 inches × 1 foot.

The *Myers Cot endowed by a bequest from Mrs Jane Cheriton. Doulton.*
Hickory Dickory Dock.

The *Edith Margaret Henderson Cot endowed by bequest of Miss Judith Henderson of Rock Ferry 14th February 1909. Doulton and Co., Lambeth.*
Three Blind Mice.

Cot endowed by Mr and Mrs O. Harrison Williams in memory of their son Alfred Harrison. Doulton and Co., Lambeth.
Jack Horner.

The *Audley Cot, 1920. Doulton and Co., Lambeth.*
Ring a Ring of Roses.

To the ever precious memory of Frank Harrison who passed away in Bermuda, January 22nd, 1951.
Blow Wind Blow.

Cot in memory of Sir Alfred Jones K.C. M.G. Ship Owner of Liverpool was endowed in 1913 from funds left under his Will.
Ride a Cock Horse.

Cot bequest of Sir Thomas Boyden Baronet, twenty years Chairman of this Home.
I saw a ship a sailing.

Cot endowed by Ann Dean Royden of Frankly.
Hey diddle diddle.

5. In two Boys' Dormitories. Eight tile pic-

tures, each 1 foot 6 inches × 1 foot. These are in a completely different style and show little animals dressed in human clothes. Five are nursery rhymes. The full verses are painted in the top corners, and each actual picture is enclosed in a circle.

There was an old woman who lived in a shoe –
Endowed by C.F. Wolfenden Esq. of West Kirby, 1953

Polly put the kettle on –
Endowed in memory of Robert and Sybilla Dalglish, late of West Kirby, 1953

Humpty Dumpty sat on a wall –
This cot is endowed by a bequest from Rodie Macfee, 1913

Jack and Jill went up the hill –
The Dobell Cot, a thank offering from Alfred and Ellen Dobell, January 1919

Sing a song of sixpence –
The Egerton of Tatton Cot dedicated by the Freemasons of Cheshire in memory of the Right Hon. Alan de Tatton, Third Baron Egerton of Tatton, March 1922

Three are set in ovals

A schoolroom scene
The Woolcott Cot endowed by bequest of Miss Edith Woolcott of West Kirby, 1951

A seaside scene
The Pelling Cot in memory of Thomas Loud and Jessie Pelling of Fernleigh, Oxton. Endowed by their children.

Unidentified picture
The Charles Edward Ashworth Cot. Endowed by a legacy from the late Charles Edward Ashworth of Blundellsands, 1932

There is also a dedication plaque
The Cot plaques in this ward are after original designs by Molly Brett and are reproduced by courtesy of the Medici Society

THE WOOLCOTT COT
ENDOWED BY BEQUEST OF MISS EDITH WOOLCOTT OF WEST KIRBY. 1951.

BRONGLAIS HOSPITAL, NORTH ROAD, ABERYSTWYTH, DYFED

FOLK TALES – MAW

Bronglais Hospital was completed in 1939. The consulting architects were Adams, Holden and Pearson of London. There are three panels situated on a circular wall of a solarium type ward and they must have been technically difficult to manufacture. Two are horizontal and one vertical. Each is made up of sixty tiles measuring 6 × 6 inches.

The pictures are signed by Edward W. Ball 1938, the artist who was responsible for the tile pictures in St. Hilda's Hospital, Hartlepool. Bronglais is now a geriatric hospital and the tiles are in a former children's ward.

Panel 1.   DICK WHITTINGTON ON HIS WAY TO LONDON
Panel 2.   THE GOOSE THAT LAID THE GOLDEN EGG
Panel 3.   LITTLE BOY BLUE FAST ASLEEP IN A CORNFIELD

CARDIFF ROYAL INFIRMARY

THIRTY SIX PANELS OF WELSH HISTORY AND NURSERY RHYMES – SIMPSON

Cardiff Royal Infirmary in the Newport Road replaced a previous infirmary and it was formerly known as the King Edward VII Hospital. The hospital must have had a unique and most colourful display of tile pictures by W.B. Simpson and Sons, but unfortunately the majority have been plastered and painted over in recent years. It is to be hoped that some can be restored.

Their importance and originality can be judged from the illustrated descriptions published by the *Western Mail* circa 1912 from which I quote extracts. The only two beautiful panels which can still be seen show St. David and St. Non.

1.   *The William James Thomas Ward was endowed, furnished and decorated with picture tiles by the generosity of Mr William James Thomas, J.P., of Bryn Awel, Ynishir. The pictures illustrate Welsh History from the 1st to the 13th Century.*

According to the commemorative booklet the pictures *were all executed by Messrs W.B. Simpson and Sons in their studios at 99 St. Martin's Lane, London WC., from the designs of Miss Gertrude Bradley, the artist, who with Messrs. Simpson and Sons have made the work a labour of love and in its execution have given very much satisfaction to the Board of Management, the donors of the pictures, and to Col. Bruce Vaughan who suggested the motive and theme of the pictures in each Ward.*[39]

The choice of Messrs. Simpson and Sons may have been influenced by the fact that 30 to 35 years earlier the firm had executed the tile pictures depicting Scenes from the Lives of the Prophets at Cardiff Castle for the Marquis of Bute.

2.   *The John Nixon Ward was endowed, furnished, and beautified by decorative picture tiles illustrating Nursery Rhymes, by Mrs John Nixon, in affectionate memory of her husband, the late John Nixon, J.P., pioneer of the development of the South Wales Steam Coal Industry.*

The artist for this set of pictures was Philip H. Newman, who also designed the tile pictures in 1898 for Bedford General Hospital.

3. The Coronation Ward commemorative booklets tells us that:—
This Ward, by the unanimous resolve of the Board of Management was named the Coronation Ward and commemorates the Coronation of their Majesties King George V and Queen Mary, on 22nd June 1911, and the Investiture of His Royal Highness Edward, Prince of Wales, at Caernarvon Castle, on 13th July 1911. The Ward has been beautified by decorative tile pictures illustrative of the Coronation and Investiture, the gifts of ladies and gentlemen, whose names are written on the respective panels.[40]

Miss Gertrude Bradley was the artist responsible for the design of the pictures which include the Princess Victoria receiving the news of the death of William IV, the Coronation of King George V and the *Presentation of the first Prince of Wales by King Edward I, 1282.*

CORONATION WARD

1. *PRINCESS VICTORIA, AFTERWARDS VICTORIA THE GOOD, WHOSE ACCESSION TO THE THRONE 1837 SYNCHRONISES WITH THE FOUNDATION OF THIS HOSPITAL. W.J. TATTEN, HIGH SHERIFF OF GLAMORGAN 1911 – 1912.*
   The picture shows the Lord Chamberlain announcing the news of her accession to young Victoria.
2. *THE CORONATION. TO HIM HIS PEOPLE COME WITH THEIR BURDENS THAT HE MAY UNBIND AND SET THEM FREE. GOD SAVE THE KING.*
   The King is shown on his throne receiving his people from overseas, women and children, and a soldier, sailor and a miner.
3. *PRESENTATION OF EDWARD PRINCE OF WALES BY KING GEORGE V. 1911. GOD BLESS THE PRINCE OF WALES. T. Lynn Thomas C.B.*
   The King and Queen Mary are seen presenting the young Prince to the people of Wales at Caernarvon Castle on 13 July 1911.
4. *PRESENTATION OF THE FIRST PRINCE OF WALES BY KING EDWARD I, 1282. Iwen John Maclean M.D.*
   The King is shown holding the infant Prince cradled on a shield with Good Queen Eleanor the mother in the background.

5. *SPIRITUAL POWER. KING OF KINGS, LORD OF LORDS, THE ONLY RULER OF PRINCES. Elize Nixon.*
A picture of Christ with the Lamp as the Light of the World, the Orb and the Crown. Purity, Truth, Love and Wisdom were symbolised in the colours of his robes – white, blue, crimson and gold.

6. *TEMPORAL POWER. THERE IS NONE OTHER THAT FIGHTETH FOR US BUT ONLY THOU, O GOD. Major General H.H. Lee J.P.*
Britannia is shown as the Guardian of the Orb, the Sceptre and the Crown.

7. *THE LEGEND OF THE CONSECRATION OF WESTMINSTER ABBEY AD.616. W. James Thomas J.P.*

8. *KENNETH MACALPINE FINDING THE STONE OF DESTINY A.D.850. W. James Thomas. J.P.*

9. *THE LEGEND OF THE OIL AND AMPULLA. W. James Thomas. J.P.*
The Virgin Mary is shown appearing to Thomas Becket at Sens.

10. *THE LEGEND OF THE KING'S WEDDING RING OF ENGLAND. W. James Thomas J.P.*
The picture tells the story of Edward the Confessor giving his ring to a poor old man. The ring was later given to two English pilgrims in Palestine by a beggar revealing himself as John the Evangelist who told them to take it back to England.

THE WILLIAM JAMES THOMAS WARD

All panels given by W. James Thomas J.P.

1. *CARADOC INCITING THE SILURES TO RESIST THE ROMANS 1st CENTURY.*
2. *ST ILLTYD TEACHING HIS PEOPLE AN IMPROVED METHOD OF PLOUGHING 5th CENTURY.*
3. *KING ARTHUR CROWNED AT CAERLEON ON USK 6th CENTURY.*
4. *ST TEILO SECOND BISHOP OF LLANDAFF 6th CENTURY. ARISE AND GO OVERSEAS.*
5. *MORGAN MWYNVAWR. HE INSTITUTED TRIAL BY JURY 8th CENTURY.*
6. *THE HOME OF A WELSH CHIEFTAIN IN THE 10th CENTURY.*
7. *MORGAN OF COYTY OFFERING ASSAR*

TEMPORAL POWER.
THERE IS NONE OTHER THAT FIGHTETH FOR US BUT ONLY THOU, O GOD. Major General H.H. Lee J.P.

HIS DAUGHTER IN MARRIAGE TO PAYN TURBERVILLE 11th CENTURY.

8. *WILLIAM THE CONQUEROR PASSING BY CARDIFF ON HIS PILGRIMAGE TO ST. DAVIDS 11th CENTURY.*
9. *ROBERT CONSUL SECOND EARL OF GLOUCESTER AT CARDIFF 12th CENTURY.*
10. *IVOR BACH WITH HIS WARRIORS SCALING THE WALLS OF CARDIFF CASTLE 12th CENTURY.*
11. *GERALD THE WELSHMAN AT CARDIFF WITH ARCHBISHOP BALDWIN 13th CENTURY.*
12. *LLEWELLYN BREN SURRENDERING HIMSELF TO SAVE HIS MEN FROM THE NORMANS 13th CENTURY.*

IN A SIDE WARD

1. *ST DAVID.*
   Painted in bright colours. St. David is in Bishop's robes preaching to his people. (colour plate)
2. *ST NON.*
   The mother of St David standing by a rock in a woodland.

THE JOHN NIXON WARD

The ward was endowed and the panels given by Mrs John Nixon in memory of her husband. A commemorative booklet shows that the pictures are identical to the series in Bedford General Hospital.[41]

1. *WHITTINGTON AND HIS CAT*
2. *CINDERELLA AND THE GLASS SHOE*
3. *DICKORY DOCK*
4. *SEE SAW*
5. *JACK HORNER*
6. *MISTRESS MARY*
7. *MISS MUFFET*
8. *JACK AND JILL*
9. *RIDE A COCK HORSE*
10. *BO-PEEP*
11. *SIMPLE SIMON*
12. *SING O' SIXPENCE*

LLANELLI GENERAL HOSPITAL

NURSERY RHYMES – DOULTON

The foundation stone of Llanelli General Hospital was laid by Mrs William Thomas on 18 October 1884 and the hospital was opened on 20 November 1885 by Mrs Rowland Maclaran. A new hospital is now being built nearby and the Hospital Authorities are anxious to save the tile pictures when the old hospital closes. They have sought the advice of the staff of Ironbridge Gorge Museum and asked the Curator of the Carmarthen Museum to compile a report on the history and condition of the pictures. The following is an extract from the report –

> *The Doulton tile panels used to decorate the children's ward of Llanelli Hospital were commissioned by Mrs H.C. Buckley as a memorial to her husband, Henry Child Buckley. Henry Child Buckley was the son of James Buckley, Penyfai, a former High Sheriff of Carmarthen. . . He was educated in Llanelli and studied medicine in London and Aberdeen. Henry Buckley later returned to Llanelli as Medical Officer of Health. . .*

A commemorative plaque by Doulton is is inscribed –

IN LOVING MEMORY OF
HENRY CHILD BUCKLEY M. D.
THIS WARD WAS ERECTED BY
HIS WIFE
OCT. 1904

The Museum Curator made four recommendations:–

1. *That the panels be preserved in situ for their historical, artistic and economic value.*
2. *If the Hospital is sold off the new owner should be offered the tiling.*
3. *Expert techniques should be used and the panels re-sited in the new hospital.*
4. *They could be offered to a Museum and Carmarthen would be glad to have them.*[42]

Each Panel consists of three parts:–

At the top a row of plain greenish tiles framed by a two inch border. In the middle, eight rows of four six inch tiles form the actual picture, and at the bottom framed in four rows of tiles, is the wording of the title between two Art Nouveau style flowers.

1. *OLD MOTHER HUBBARD. M.E. Thompson Doulton & Co., Ltd. Lambeth S.E.*
2. *JACK AND JILL. M.E. Thompson Doulton & Co., Ltd. Lambeth S.E.*
3. *LITTLE JACK HORNER. M.E. Thompson Doulton & Co., Ltd. Lambeth S.E.*
4. *DING DONG BELL. M.E. Thompson Doulton & Co., Ltd. Lambeth S.E.*
5. *LITTLE BOY BLUE. M.E. Thompson Doulton & Co., Ltd. Lambeth S.E.*
6. *SEE SAW MARGERY DAW. M.E. Thompson Doulton & Co., Ltd. Lambeth S.E.*
7. *LITTLE MISS MUFFET. M.E. Thompson Doulton & Co., Ltd. Lambeth S.E.*
8. LOST DURING WARD ALTERATIONS.
9. LOST DURING WARD ALTERATIONS.

MAESTEG GENERAL HOSPITAL, MAESTEG, WEST GLAMORGAN

A TILE FRIEZE – CARTER

Maesteg began as a small Miners' General Hospital in 1916 and as so often happens in South Wales, the money for it was mostly raised from contributions made by the miners of the area. A children's ward was added in 1926 and the tiling completed in 1936.

The pictures are bright and colourful and depict animals in human clothing painted on a frieze, two six inch tiles in height and varying in length according to the structure of the ward. Each panel is framed in a dark blue tiled border two inches wide. In addition there are two large pictures – The Old Woman who lived in a Shoe, and The Ark. The work is typical of Carters and many of the pictures are illustrated in their 1930s catalogue advertising tile pictures for hospitals.

1. THE OLD WOMAN WHO LIVED IN A SHOE. 6 × 4 feet.
2. A DUCK WEARING A BOW TIE AND A YELLOW HAT. 1 × 1 foot.
3. AN ALLIGATOR WEARING RED SHOES, DARK TROUSERS, AND A BLUE JACKET WITH YELLOW COLLAR. 2 × 1 feet.

Several panels follow on the same lines ending up with the impression of the animals heading for the large picture of the Ark at the end of the Ward.

4. THE ARK AT ANCHOR, A LADDER AT THE SIDE AND TWO CREW MEN STANDING ON THE BOW. 6 × 4 feet.

TALYGARN REHABILITATION CENTRE, MID GLAMORGAN

Talygarn Mansion and 100 acre estate was purchased in 1923 by the South Wales Miners District Welfare Committee and in October that year it became the Talygarn Miners' Convalescent Home.[43] Previous owners had furnished the house with rare panelling and carving, painted ceilings, Carrara marble mantelpieces and extensive areas of tiling. The grounds were planted with ornamental trees and shrubs and the whole environment must have been an ideal place for convalescence for members of the mining community.

In 1943 Talygarn changed from a Convalescent Home to a Rehabilitation Centre for injured miners, mostly cases with fractured limbs suffered in the coal industry. It was subsequently taken over by the National Health Service and administered by the Mid Glamorgan Health Authority.

TILE FEATURES – MAINLY 17th and 18th CENTURY DELFT TILES AND ITALIAN TILE PICTURES.

1. Entrance Hall. Fireplace richly decorated with Manganese Delft.
2. Inner Hall. Little fireplace. Blue and White Delft. Country Scenes surrounded by circles and stylised flowers within diamonds.
3. Great Hall. Large fireplace with a mixture of blue and white, manganese and polychrome tiles.
4. Two Bedrooms. Large fireplaces most sensibly made into cupboards with all manganese and blue and white tiles retained and visible when the doors are opened.
5. Winter Garden. (Conservatory). Six heraldic panels each of six tiles with moulded borders. Italian Majolica.
   One panel shows a Lion.? Venetian.
   Two panels 6 feet × 3 feet 9 inches depict battle scenes. One is a copy of a war mosaic from the House of the Faun in Pompeii taken from a Greek wall painting of 300 BC., with Alexander the Great in a battle against the Persian Emperor Darius the Third.[44]

ROYAL GWENT HOSPITAL, NEWPORT

SIX INCH TILE PICTURES, NURSERY RHYMES – MAKER UNKNOWN

The Royal Gwent Hospital dates from 2 August 1897 when the foundation stone was laid by Lord Tredegar. It was opened in 1901 as the Newport and County Infirmary and renamed the Royal Gwent in 1913.

In a side ward of what was previously a general surgical ward, the walls are tiled from floor to ceiling in plain white. About four feet from the ground is a row of six inch tile pictures alternating with the white tiles. Twelve popular rhymes have been used and they have been repeated to make an approximate total of eighty tile pictures.

The hospital staff are very interested in their tiles and they are also much appreciated by the patients. It is hoped that they will be preserved when the ward is eventually closed.

THE PICTURES

1. RIDE A COCK HORSE TO BANBURY CROSS.
2. HEY DIDDLE DIDDLE THE CAT AND THE FIDDLE.
3. DICKORY DOCK THE MOUSE RAN UP THE CLOCK.
4. JACK AND JILL WENT UP THE HILL.
5. JACK FELL DOWN AND BROKE HIS CROWN.
6. LITTLE BO-PEEP HAS LOST HER SHEEP.

7. BAA BAA BLACK SHEEP.
8. MARY HAD A LITTLE LAMB.
9. DING DONG BELL, PUSSY'S IN THE WELL.
10. WHO PULLED HIM OUT, LITTLE JOHNNY STOUT.
11. WHERE ARE YOU GOING MY PRETTY MAID.
12. LITTLE JACK HORNER.

THE ROYAL BELFAST HOSPITAL FOR SICK CHILDREN

NURSERY RHYMES, FAIRY TALES, CHILDREN'S PASTIMES, AND BIBLICAL SCENES – MINTON HOLLINS

When the previous Children's Hospital was being built in 1879, Florence Nightingale wrote to the Matron, Miss Lennox, asking for a tracing of the plans for the Grand Duchess of Baden who was involved in a Children's Hospital project in Heidelberg and wanted plans of the best new hospitals.[45]

The present hospital was opened in April 1932 on a site in the Falls Road. The very good tile pictures are in two wards. Barbour has 14 and Musgrave 13 panels, and all carry the names of the donors. One has the signature Anne M Yeames, who was presumably the artist or designer of the pictures, which are different in style from all others I have seen. The manufacture was attributed to Doultons, but my researches led me to the firm of MacNaughton and Blair who as Norman MacNaughton and Sons, Builders Merchants, gave four of the pictures. A member of the firm sent me information from a former employee:

> The tiles were manufactured by Minton Hollins of Stoke-on-Trent. The tiles were supplied and fixed by Norman MacNaughton and Sons Ltd. The donors wished to have the tiles painted locally but Mintons preferred to have the work done by people who were used to the type of decoration. Mintons submitted a number of sketches to the Committee who chose the required number after which I think the tiles were painted at the Works.

The Hospital is justifiably proud of its tile pictures. All are 5 feet × 3 feet 6 inches.

1. *THE SWING The Junior Committee*
2. *ORANGES AND LEMONS A Child Lover*
3. *PAPER BOATS Causeway 1931*
4. *SUMMER Mr and Mrs J.S. Morrow*
5. *LITTLE BO-PEEP Deirdre Mary Davison*
6. *DAVID WATCHING HIS FATHER'S SHEEP Peter Clark*
7. *DICK WHITTINGTON Mrs D.C. Lindsay*
8. *THE FLIGHT INTO EGYPT Colin Clark*
9. *LITTLE TOM TUCKER Edna R. McAuley*
10. *WINTER McNeile McCormack*
11. *JACK AND JILL Honor Atkinson*
12. *RIDE A COCK HORSE Inez M.G. Robinson*
13. *RAIN, RAIN GO AWAY Ladies Committee 1930*
14. *DING DONG BELL Gwendoline M.A. Robinson*
15. *THE HOUSE THAT JACK BUILT The Misses Paul*
16. *MARY MARY QUITE CONTRARY Ursula Adelaide Totton*
17. *BY THE SEA Norman MacNaughton & Sons Ltd*
18. *THE MOUSE RAN UP THE CLOCK Walter J. Richardson Esq. Hon Treasurer 1931*
19. *THE NEW BALL Mrs. Charlotte Grainger*
20. *LITTLE BOY BLUE Norman MacNaughton & Sons Ltd*
21. *THE FINDING OF MOSES Tony Clark*
22. *THE ADORATION OF THE MAGI Beatrice Clark*
23. *CINDERELLA Mrs G.G. McCrea*
24. *MARY HAD A LITTLE LAMB Norman MacNaughton & Sons Ltd*
25. *SPRINGTIME Norman MacNaughton & Sons Ltd*
26. *THE GOOSE GIRL Mrs T.D. Paul*
27. *SIMPLE SIMON Thomas D. Paul*

THE ROYAL EDINBURGH SICK CHILDREN'S HOSPITAL, SCIENNES ROAD, EDINBURGH

NURSERY RHYMES, FAIRY TALES AND COUNTRY SCENES – DOULTON

The Royal Edinburgh Sick Children's Hospital was built in 1895. In the unusual setting of the Anaesthetic Room by the old operating theatre are some delightful tile pictures painted in blue and white instead of the popular polychrome. I imagine the room must formerly have been a children's side ward, because the anaesthetic equipment has been fitted to the wall through one of the tile panels.

1. *PUSS IN BOOTS*. Puss presents a rabbit to the King. The picture differs substantially from the same subject in St. Thomas' Hospital and is an example of how the Doulton orders were individually produced for their different customers. One small touch is the inclusion of the Scottish Thistle in the picture. 4 × 2 feet.

2. *CURLY LOCKS*. Only the title is included whereas the Newcastle Royal Infirmary has the full verse. 4 × 2 feet.

3. A long narrow wall panel showing six dancers, fiddler and flute player dressed in 17th Century costume in an open air idyllic setting. A jug of ale stands on the ground nearby. As two haycocks can be seen in the background perhaps it is a harvest dance. 6 feet 6 inches × 1 foot 6 inches.

4. A country scene with a windmill and a field of sheep. 1 foot 6 inches × 6 inches.

5. A country cottage with a lady by the garden gate and hens in the foreground. 1 foot 6 inches × 6 inches.

BALLAMONA HOSPITAL, ISLE OF MAN

SINGLE TILES OF NURSERY RHYMES ETC – MAW

Ballamona Hospital was opened in 1868 and some additions were made in the 1880s. The tile pictures are in a part of the hospital which is now used as a School of Nursing. They are particularly interesting because they appear to be designed by Walter Crane for Maw and Co., c. 1878 – 1880 but are unsigned. They are in attractive colours and represent well known nursery rhymes. I was recently told that only a few sets of these are known. Fortunately the Ballamona tiles are in situ though they narrowly missed being removed.

In addition to the Nursery Rhymes there are four tiles representing the ancient elements, *Terra*, *Acqua*, *Ignis* and *Zephyria*. The pictures were hand painted and Maws have a description of the designs and the technique used by the artist.

Walter Crane 1845 – 1915 is best known for his illustrations of children's books in the Victorian era.

THE TILES

All 6 × 6 inches

1. *MISTRESS MARY*
2. *LITTLE BROWN BETTY*
3. *LITTLE BO-PEEP*
4. *LITTLE BOY BLUE*
5. *TOM TUCKER*
6. *JOCK HE WAS A PIPER'S SON*
7. Single tiles with a stylised leaf and flower design separate the nursery rhymes.
8. *TERRA*
9. *IGNIS*
10. *ZEPHYRIA*
11. *ACQUA*

8, 9, 10 and 11, the ancient elements, are represented by classical figures.

LITTLE
BO: PEEP.

ST. HELIER MATERNITY HOSPITAL, ST. HELIER, JERSEY, C.I.

TWO TILE PICTURES – CARTER

In the former Children's Ward of the present Maternity Hospital there are two tile panels measuring four feet by three feet. They are painted in pastel colours and are the only ones of their kind found during the period of this study.

One picture represents Christ blessing children and the second appears to be a girl coming upon a fairy wedding witnessed by elves and a hare beside two large mushrooms in a forest. Both pictures are signed *Carters Poole 1925* and the initials *J.R.Y.* The artist James Radley Young joined Carters soon after the turn of the century and in addition to his work as an artist and designer, he became well known as a trainer of the many girls who learned the skills of pottery painting at Carters. His name is prominent in the history of the Poole Pottery Company by Jennifer Hawkins.

1. CHRIST RECEIVING CHILDREN
2. ELF KING AND FAIRIES

THE SASSOON HOSPITAL, POONA, INDIA

NURSERY RHYMES AND FAIRY TALES – DOULTON

An item in the *Royal Doulton International Collectors Club Journal* describes a visit by a Mr Angus Lindsay to the Sassoon Hospital in Poona.[46] In the E N T Ward, formerly for children, he found six panels of nursery rhymes and five fairy tales all signed *M.E. Thompson, Doulton and Co., Lambeth SE*. The building was paid for by Sir Jacob Sassoon and opened on 15 March 1909.

Mr Lindsay found a long and vivid account of the opening ceremony in *The Times of India*; bands played and five hundred guests were present to hear speeches in a large marquee. Lady Sassoon was quoted as taking the keenest of interest in the progress of the building, *the greater part of which was Minton tiled*. This was presumably plain tiling, for the account goes on to say that *a most touching feature in the present building is the brightening of the Children's Wards a thought inspired by her Ladyship*.

Four of the panels can be identified from photographs.

1. CINDERELLA IN THE KITCHEN.
2. THE FAIRY SENDING CINDERELLA TO THE BALL.
3. PUSS IN BOOTS.
4. JACK AND JILL.

SOUTHLAND HOSPITAL, KEW, INVERCARGILL, NEW ZEALAND

A FRIEZE OF NURSERY RHYMES – THYNNE

In rescuing old records from the derelict Victoria Tile Works in Hereford during my wife's research into the history of the Hereford tile makers, we came across an interesting advertising leaflet produced by the firm of H. & G. Thynne of Hereford which stated:–

> *IN A CHILDREN'S WARD*
> *In a New Zealand Hospital it was planned to have a double frieze of glazed tile pictures above the little beds. The conditions were not easy. The frieze is interrupted by windows and doors, and broken by partitions that form cubicles, each containing two beds. Over each bed are short sections of wall, each holding two panels. The size of the panels varies from under two feet to over six feet – the larger ones being at the sides of the doors on each end wall.*
> *NURSERY RHYMES*
> *or similar subjects were decided on by the Architect. Thynnes after a careful examination of the problem, decided that there were subjects in verse, and some few in prose like Aesop's Fables, that could be added. Many hundreds were collected and studied. All those that contained ideas or words that might not be helpful to the eye and mind of a sick child were excluded, and all those that could help the nurses and cheer the patients were collected.*
> *These were arranged in groups, planned in harmony of colour, line and idea. A full list of all the suggested verses and pictures was submitted. The order was placed and has been executed.*[47]

A newspaper cutting from the *Invercargill Evening News* dated 19 March 1937 was also found.[48] It showed photographs of the tile pictures in position and told a vivid story of the controversy that surrounded the choice of a site for the hospital. A happier item however mentioned the raising of £220 by a group of children called Little Southlanders for the nursery rhyme tile pictures.

Correspondence with Miss Rachel Peek, Principal Nurse at the hospital in 1982, confirmed that the tile murals are still there and treasured by patients and staff alike. She also supplied photographs of the tiles, the only ones of this kind to my knowledge which were made for any hospital at home or abroad. The titles were decorated by the tube-lining process.

NURSERY RHYMES etc. APPEARING ON THE PHOTOGRAPHS

TOM TOM THE PIPER'S SON
TOMMY TUCKER SINGING FOR HIS SUPPER
SIMPLE SIMON MET A PIE MAN
ALICE IN WONDERLAND
DOCTOR FOSTER WENT TO GLOUCESTER
HOW MANY MILES TO BABYLON
LITTLE JACK HORNER
COCK A DOODLE
OLD KING COLE
MISTRESS MARY
SING A SONG OF SIXPENCE
HEY DIDDLE DIDDLE
THERE WAS AN OLD WOMAN WHO LIVED IN
A SHOE
THIS LITTLE PIG WENT TO MARKET
WOMAN WENT UP IN A BASKET
I SAW A SHIP A SAILING
LITTLE MISS MUFFET (colour plate)
SEE SAW MARGERY DAW

THE WELLINGTON HOSPITAL, NEWTOWN, WELLINGTON, NEW ZEALAND

NURSERY RHYMES AND FAIRY TALES – DOULTON

Wellington Hospital is included in these records because the tile pictures were made in England and it is an example of how the fashions at home extended to hospitals overseas. The hospital had an exciting beginning because of a public row between a *Presbyterian Minister of Religion* and an *Actor Producer of Saucy Plays*.[49] In supporting the appeal for the building funds the actor was getting publicity for his theatre productions while the Minister was busily condemning the plays as satanic. When all the money was collected there was £800 in excess of what was needed and it was then decided to purchase tile murals by Doultons for the decoration of the children's ward. The pictures are attributed to the artists Margaret Thompson and William Rowe.[50]

In 1982 Miss G.A. Grattan, Principal Nurse, told me that the tile pictures were highly prized and everybody was interested in preserving them. As a result of our correspondence the hospital produced greetings cards with pictures of the nursery rhymes and fairy tales.

Professor H.J. Weston, Head of Department of Paediatrics, wrote in 1985 asking for comments as the seventy year old children's wards were due for closure in three years' time and he was concerned about the future of the tile pictures. I wrote to New Zealand House, and also asked Heritage Tile Conservation to advise Professor Weston. I understand that Royal Doulton have been consulted and may help in some way.

1. *SEE SAW MARGERY DAW.*
2. *OLD MOTHER HUBBARD.*
3. *CINDERELLA.*
4. *MARY MARY QUITE CONTRARY.*
5. *HERE WE COME GATHERING NUTS IN MAY.*
6. *DING DONG BELL.*
7. *OLD KING COLE.*
8. *SING A SONG O SIXPENCE.*
9. *LITTLE BO-PEEP.*
10. *SIMPLE SIMON MET A PIEMAN.*
11. *SIMPLE SIMON WENT A FISHING.*
12. *PUSS IN BOOTS. 1.*
13. *PUSS IN BOOTS. 2.*
14. *RED RIDING HOOD.*
15. *HANSEL AND GRETEL.*
16. *HEY DIDDLE DIDDLE.*
17. *RED RIDING HOOD.*

(List of panels kindly sent by Miss Grattan)

RECENT INFORMATION

BRIDGEWATER GENERAL HOSPITAL had tiles supplied by CARTERS, probably in the nineteen thirties when the hospital was extended, but unfortunately they were removed during alterations to the Children's Ward in the 1970s. The scheme included the 6 inch Nursery Rhymes and Nursery Toys series designed by Dora Batty in 1921 − 29, and the Coloured Dutch series designed by Joseph Roelants in 1921 − 28.

THE ROYAL FREE HOSPITAL in Grays Inn Road, London, suffered damage during the Second World War and is now closed. Nothing remains of the Dora Batty Nursery Rhyme series of 6 inch tile pictures supplied in 1935 by CARTERS for the Children's Ward.

A sales leaflet of the firm W.B. SIMPSON & SONS mentions the supply of tiles to CHELTENHAM GENERAL HOSPITAL. Nursing staff remember the tiles in the former Children's Ward in the East Block, built in 1936, but cannot recall details of the pictures. The tiles were destroyed during alterations in the early nineteen seventies.

The new WESTON SUPER MARE GENERAL HOSPITAL which opened in September 1986 has a tiled picture of the earlier (1928) Queen Alexandra Memorial Hospital. It was commissioned by the Bristol and Weston Health Authority who, together with the architect and the artist, are to be congratulated on producing this imaginative tile scheme to enhance the attractive architecture of this very modern hospital

The picture, 3 feet 6 inches × 10 feet, is the work of local artist Rosie Smith, using on-glaze enamels on H & R JOHNSON Crystal tile blanks. It is framed and fixed to a wall in the main entrance hall, and will be partnered later in the year by a picture of Weston Super Mare Winter Gardens.

NOTES AND REFERENCES

1. Robertson B.M. and Cave S.W. 'The Lord Mayor Treloar Hospital'. *News sheet of the British Association of Orthopaedic Nurses*, March 1972.
2. Bedford County Hospital. A commemorative booklet, circa 1898.
3. Atterbury, Paul and Irvine. *The Doulton Story*, souvenir booklet for an exhibition at the Victoria and Albert Museum, London, 1979.
4. Coleshill Hall Hospital. A handbook of hospital affairs.
5. *Derbyshire Children's Hospital 1877–1977*, a commemorative booklet.
6. Van Lemmem, Hans. *Minton Hollins Picture Tiles*, Gladstone Pottery Museum 1984, revised 1985.
7. Some historical notes on Garston Manor.
8. Summerbell, C.T. A souvenir sketch of the Hartlepool Hospital 1865 – 1948.
9. History of the West Wing, Hemel Hempstead Hospital. Historical note.
10. Greene, Betty. 'The Godwins of Hereford', *Journal of the Tiles and Architectural Society* Vol 1, 1982, 8 – 16.
11. An inventory of the Delft tiles, St. Bartholomew's Hospital.
12. Bolingbroke Hospital 1880 – 1980. A centenary booklet.
13. Cheyne Centre for Spastic Children. Publicity brochure.
14. Notes on the history of the Central Middlesex Hospital.
15. *Nursery Rhyme Book*. A souvenir of the Princess Elizabeth Ward, Ealing Hospital, 1934.
16. The King's Fund Miniature Hospital souvenir exhibition booklet, 1933.
17. W.B. Simpson & Sons, *Tiles supplied to hospitals*, undated trade leaflet.
18. Paddington Green Children's Hospital. Annual reports, 1895 – 1912.
19. *Pictures in Pottery*. A note on some recent hospital wall decorations executed by Doulton & Co, Lambeth, London SE, 1904, p 13.
20. Catleugh, Jon. *William De Morgan Tiles*, Trefoil Books, 1983.
21. A short history of St. Mary's Hospital, Praed Street, London.
22. St. Mary's Hospital, Plaistow, London. Annual reports 1921 – 22.
23. Curry, Mary. 'Lilian, a Profile'. *Nightingale Fellowship Journal* XI no 103, July 1980, 86 – 88.
24. *St. Thomas' Hospital Gazettes*, Summer 1980, 1982.
25. 'Westminster Hospital. Under the Shadow of the Abbey', *Nursing Mirror* 11 November 1938.
26. *Guide*. News items, 1923, 24, 25.
27. 'The Medmenham Pottery'. *Glazed Expressions* No 6, 1986. Tiles and Architectural Ceramics Society.
28. Newspaper files in Newcastle upon Tyne City Library.
29. Austwick, J. and B. *The Decorated Tile*, Pitman House, 1980.
30. *The Builder*, 5 December 1863.
31. *Portsmouth News* 13 February 1980.
32. Borocourt Hospital, publicity booklet.
33. A short history of Stamford and Rutland Hospital 1829–1978.
34. Payne, F.J. *The History of Torbay Hospital 1844–1980*.
35. *The Kent and Sussex Courier*, August 1904.
36. *Carter Picture Tiles for Hospitals*, advertising brochure, c 1935.
37. Hawkins, Jennifer. *The Poole Potteries*, Barrie and Jenkins, London 1980.
38. Archives of West Kirby Residential School, 1981.
39, 40, 41. *The King Edward VII's Hospital, Cardiff*, Western Mail Ltd., Cardiff. Commemorative booklets. *c*. 1912.

42. The Doulton tile panels in Llanelli Hospital. Carmarthen Museum.
43. *The Miner* August 1946.
44. Wheeler, Mortimer. *Roman Art and Architecture* Thames & Hudson 1944.
45. McCreary, Alf. *The Royal Belfast Hospital for Sick Children, One hundred years of caring 1873–1973*, Belfast 1973.
46. Lindsay, Angus. *Journal of the Royal Doulton International Collectors Club* 1981.
47. *Can Do.* Advertising leaflet c 1937.
48. *The Invercargill Evening News* 19 March 1937.
49. *The Journal of the Wellington Hospital Board*, No 5 March 1982.
50. Irvine Louise. *The Journal of the Royal Doulton I.C. Club* 1981.